Praise for *Numbers and Sense: Ensuring Student Success One Cohort at a Time*

"*Numbers and Sense: Ensuring Student Success One Cohort at a Time* provides a synthesis of lessons learned and challenges faced in higher education. There are questions to ponder, technologies to consider, and a great deal of resources. Alexandra Salas also brings to life the voices of successful thought leaders in higher education."

—**Yesenia Madas**, associate vice president, Student Affairs, Brookdale Community College

"*Numbers and Sense* includes the insights and perspectives of numerous educators as to why ensuring student success requires a comprehensive and holistic approach. Salas provides reflective and actionable recommendations for what needs to be done to lead change."

—**Tia Brown McNair**, EdD, vice president for diversity, equity, and student success, AACU

"Salas' book is required reading for community college leaders, faculty, and staff. No college can claim it is 'student-centered' without implementing the recommendations in this book. Salas not only offers crucially important insights about who today's community college students really are, but she also sets forth a practical guide for achieving student success based on her current front-line experience. Read *Numbers and Sense*, then take it to your next meeting or retreat."

—**Mark W. Rocha**, executive vice president, Cardenio Consulting, Higher Education Practice and former California community college president

"In *Numbers and Sense*, Salas provides an important new resource for those concerned about student success. Understanding the need for higher education institutions to change, develop, and evolve to remain relevant, Salas outlines relevant pathways for those interested in updating their mindset on advising, teaching, and enrollment strategies. In today's volatile, uncertain, complex, and ambiguous global marketplace now marked by a pandemic creating seismic forces higher education will need to deal with for years to come, Salas offers a reliable blueprint to consider for those willing to update their institutional missions and create the change necessary to prepare students for their future."

—**Michael Edmondson**, dean, College of Professional Studies,
New Jersey City University and author of
Agility: Management Principles for A Volatile World

"Salas's *Numbers and Sense* is one of the first books to uniquely raise awareness, questions, and suggestions based on today's rapidly changing learning demands to ensure student success. This book elucidates Salas's assertion, 'These are exciting times as a new normal provisions to engage, and support students toward success like never before . . . one cohort at a time!'

—**Steven J. Bassett**, PhD, director of academic affairs,
USAF Expeditionary Operations School

"In this book, Salas shares many of the challenges facing community colleges today and communicates a sense of urgency for action to increase student success. Throughout this book, she brings the reader numerous stories of how current community college leaders are engaging in bold and much-needed actions to move the needle on student success. Her commitment to and passion for student success is clearly evident!"

—**Christine Harrington**, PhD, associate professor and co-coordinator; EdD
in Community College Leadership New Jersey City University

"Salas offers us a very clear and transparent twenty-first-century hands on approach to advising and student success coaching that takes the fullest advantage of both high tech and high touch methods at a time and a day when both have become essential. Few have the skills and patience to command both aspects of teaching, advising, and student coaching, but Salas offers a qualitative balance between Them. . . . This book offers a first-hand insight into what the best practices of student success coaching involve in the second decade of the twenty-first century."

—**Joseph Cronin**, chair, Individualized Master of Arts Program,
Antioch University

Numbers and Sense

Numbers and Sense

Ensuring Student Success One Cohort at a Time

Alexandra Salas

ROWMAN & LITTLEFIELD
Lanham • Boulder • New York • London

Published by Rowman & Littlefield
An imprint of The Rowman & Littlefield Publishing Group, Inc.
4501 Forbes Boulevard, Suite 200, Lanham, Maryland 20706
www.rowman.com

6 Tinworth Street, London SE11 5AL, United Kingdom

Copyright © 2021 by Alexandra Salas

All rights reserved. No part of this book may be reproduced in any form or by any electronic or mechanical means, including information storage and retrieval systems, without written permission from the publisher, except by a reviewer who may quote passages in a review.

British Library Cataloguing in Publication Information Available

Library of Congress Cataloging-in-Publication Data

Names: Salas, Alexandra, 1967- author.
Title: Numbers and sense : ensuring student success one cohort at a time / Alexandra Salas.
Description: Lanham : Rowman & Littlefield, [2021] | Includes bibliographical references. | Summary: "This book includes cases and interviews with thought leaders who candidly share experiences and realizations about ensuring student success"— Provided by publisher.
Identifiers: LCCN 2020050566 (print) | LCCN 2020050567 (ebook) | ISBN 9781475855364 (cloth) | ISBN 9781475855371 (paperback) | ISBN 9781475855388 (epub)
Subjects: LCSH: Academic achievement. | Motivation in education.
Classification: LCC LB1062.6 .S27 2021 (print) | LCC LB1062.6 (ebook) | DDC 370.15/4—dc23
LC record available at https://lccn.loc.gov/2020050566
LC ebook record available at https://lccn.loc.gov/2020050567

Dedication
To my success coaches: my mother, my uncle, my aunt, and my father, who is always with me.

Contents

Foreword: From Success Coaches — xi

Preface — xiii

Acknowledgments — xv

1 Advising Architects — 1

2 Assessing Enrollment Realities — 15

3 Financial Mindset for Student Success — 21

4 Retention 4.0: Disruptors, Adapters, Adopters — 31

5 Agency and Change — 41

6 Mission Accomplishing — 49

Education Resource Guide — 85

Bibliography — 93

About the Author — 99

Foreword

From Success Coaches

"Hey Coach, I really need you; no one else can help me." This is a statement heard over and over again in my office, in the hallway, walking across campus . . . . I know that I am not the only one who can assist this student but we have built a relationship based on trust that I won't let him down. There may be several people who can help, but he doesn't know who they are or where to find them. I reply to him, "It's ok, I got a guy." That guy might be a girl, but I know to whom we need to speak or what we need to do to resolve this student's issue.

Success coaching is founded on a holistic, proactive, and transformational approach that gives the right tools to the students in order for them to become confident in their abilities for success. It is about active listening, thoughtful questions, and creating a dialogue that allows students to share their stories. The details of the story are where the underlying challenges can be fully unearthed. The student who is struggling in math may have outside obligations that are preventing him from getting to class on time. Or the student who is reticent to get additional support through the Learning Center may just need to be told, "Ask for Chris and tell him that Killian sent you."

The idea that the student is not an anonymous entity can foster a sense of belonging, making her want to come to campus or return for more classes. That someone cares about his or her story nurtures self-efficacy—"I am college material"—and strengthens their commitment to their career goals. Understanding the myriad of services available to them may build confidence in institutional support. All of these strategies further bolster academic success while enhancing life skills. That is what a success coach does.

Nichol Killian, Former Success Coach,
Mercer County Community College

I started out as a language and career development educator. I then assumed my role as a success coach. In the beginning I looked at the responsibility as a noble thing to do, as this role in a way brings you in a full circle with your students. You're their professor in the classroom and their advisor outside of the classroom. Further down the road, I found myself falling in love with the role of a success coach and its impact on student success when I supported a program entitled the First Thirty, which focused on students on route to completing the first thirty credits of their community college journey. Later, my passion for student success is what connected me with Dr. Salas, who was the dean of a new division at Mercer County Community College: Innovation, Online Education and Student Success.

Not long after, she spearheaded the creation of a new model that focused on students' support and the integration of technology. This model married the human touch (one-on-one) with the tech advancement, and it required from the coaches to provide a specialized support for their specific divisions and other cohorts.

How is success coaching or academic advising a unique field for educators who dare to dream of a better world for their students? The very giving nature of the advising arena allows advisors—through building a **S**ustained (available every semester), **S**trategic (15 minutes is not for everyone . . . it could be more or less), **I**ntegrated (ongoing support, and advising about everything—no delegation to career, financial, or else), **P**roactive (outreach students, don't wait until issues take place), and **P**ersonalized relationship with students—to influence major changes in their attitudes, beliefs, and values to a point where their goals and visions are internalized and achieved beyond expectations (Bass, 1985; Yukl, 1999a; 1999b). The coaches are able to help students maximize their efforts by inspiring them to identify with a vision that surpasses their own immediate self-interests.

Dr. Salas ably tackles the success coaching topic as she experienced firsthand the impact of such support on students' success. She was a key player in structuring and implementing the success coaching model at our institution. Given her technology and education background, her innovative nature, and her official capacity as the lead on this project, she was the right candidate for supporting the progress and development of this advising model. For this reason, I believe that her book is a must-read for any educator who wants to learn not only about the structure or the importance of the advising model but also about the personal touch and the human impact that such model can provide its students and advisors.

Jehan Mohamed, Success Coach, Mercer County Community College

Preface

THE WHY

A middle school teacher who I came to know as my seventh-grade social studies instructor became my mentor well past high school and college, and nurtured my curiosity to learn and excel. Most importantly my mentor exemplified the critical connections between education, career, and life. And so, when I first stood before a class of college students as an adjunct instructor, and had no idea what to expect as I spent most of my life seated on other side of the podium, things clicked.

After teaching my first class, I was hooked by all the energy in the classroom generated by student questions, challenges, and bold dispositions, and it reminded me of the why: Why student success is predicated on teaching and the interactions and caring beyond the classroom.

Learning, teaching, and mentoring are intertwined ongoing elements of personal and professional growth that are maximized by an early start. At the community college there are students who despite their age and experiences may not have a support system to assist them in meeting their goals, whatever those might be. Some may not even have a clear picture of what they would like for their future. Moreover, without appropriate advising, students can overextend their time in college, incur unnecessary expenses, and not meet their expectations timely.

Based on my former experience overseeing Mercer County Community College's brand-new division of Innovation, Online Education and Student Success, formed to support organizational innovation and an agile advising structure that could meet student needs, this book offers strategies to reach and serve students: purposeful mediated technology use, cross-functional teams, and tiered advising approaches. It also presents many other perspectives gleaned from personal experience and from the experiences of other higher education professionals dedicated to student success. A work-in-progress, learning how to best serve students is an iterative process. Sharing these takeaways orbits without pretense to assist others in academia seeking to advance student success. This book examines ongoing advising challenges affecting all students that include but are not limited to first-year, international, athletes, adult learners, and online learners. Key in this is an understanding by all involved that student success is a position-agnostic campus-wide effort.

This book is as much about ensuring student success as it is about leading change one cohort at a time, illustrating courageous and dedicated voices and stewards that continue to make things happen.

Acknowledgments

Special thanks to Dr. Jianping Wang, Dr. Guy Generals, Dr. Joy Gates Black, Dr. Charlie Nutt, Dr. Darcy Hardy, Dr. Ross Markle, Simon Nynens, Nichol Killian, Jehan Mohamed, Jeff Zuckerman, Dr. Sheila Perkins, Courtney Brazile, Dr. Sharon Sherman, Dr. Oscar van den Wijngaard, Dr. Michael A. Baston, and Dr. Mark Harris.

I would also like to acknowledge the 2015–2018 core MercerOnline team (Vicente Erazo, Rodney Hargis, Jill Marcus, and Noel Quiles), whose collective genius welcomed challenges and always sought alternative solutions as members of the Division of Innovation, Online Education and Student Success, Mercer County Community College.

Chapter 1

Advising Architects

Students mean everything to higher education. Without students, silence would echo throughout brick-and-mortar and online learning spaces. Consequently, the challenge of gaining and sustaining enrollment is real, as high education leaders review like stock market analysts[1] semester after semester, year-to-date enrollment trends, dips and decline, and huddle regularly to strategize on ways to recruit and retain students. "While it can be said that retention has always been area of significance, no longer can community college lean on boom enrollment that spanned at least a decade. Looking at the numbers was always there, but now we have to be more invested in students. And the ones that show up we have to cultivate," said Dr. Ross Markle, founder and managing director of DIA Higher Education Collaborators and president of Northeastern Educational Research Association.

Needless to say, panacea for enrollment, retention, and completion challenges in higher education unveil that there is no quick-fix but rather a holistic advising approach that is a transformative change that calls for cross-functional transparency, collaboration, communication, urgency, buy-in, and courage.

Called by other names, this holistic modality is also recognized as success coaching, shared advising, intrusive advising, proactive advising, and the like. Despite the unique makeup of institutions of higher learning, the common thread that makes this kind of change attainable is the goal to ably serve students so they can achieve successful transfer to their future goals albeit gainful employment, personal enrichment, or additional education pursuits. This is a global discussion for educators and administrators and a key topic for organizations and events such as Achieving the Dream, NACADA (National Academic Advising Association—the Global Community for Academic Advising), NASPA (National Association of Student Personnel Administrators) Annual conference, the Consortium for

Student Retention Data Exchange at the University of Oklahoma (National Symposium on Student Retention), EduLearn, GlobalLearn, International Society for Technology in Education (ISTE), just to name a few.

The realization is that when data demonstrates enrollment challenges and teetering student satisfaction, change can be paralyzing option. And, despite the efforts of many who are committed to serve students, progress is thwarted by some who refuse to see the trend and still hang on to legacy, past practices, and business processes that fail to align with current systems and moves that can reverse the downward spiral taking place. So what to do? It begins with the mindset that student success and student satisfaction are the responsibility of not just a few but the whole—senior leadership, deans, directors, faculty, professional staff, support staff—everyone.

Qualitative and quantitative data can help generate invaluable predictive and descriptive analytics that can help this work. Dr. Markle, whose business provides institutions with as system that can help "connect data to action" beyond traditional data approaches, says the information gathered reveals an array of factors to help colleges better understand their students. "We don't have one group of students . . . You have to be able to distinguish . . . you can't build one system . . . if you think you are going to keep the organization the same and get different results that's impossible," notes Dr. Markle.

The idea of a one-size-fits-all system that can serve the entire student body with all its varying characteristics seems irrational. The objective of holistic advising is building a "process by which you can have individual conversations or you can segment and identify groups of students where interventions are necessary," says Dr. Markle. However, institutions must recognize that there is not just one group of students. "Whatever your population, you have that many stories that you have to impact," says Markle. From a financial perspective, which is a critical area that affects student success, the Financial Literacy and Education Commission (FLEC) also recommends needs assessments that help to gauge a students' perspective about things financial.

"The effective educator must also understand the individual and his or her unique situation and mindset. Attitude and needs assessments can help the educator and consumer identify gaps and motivations in order to customize the financial education approach. For example, the Consumer Financial Protection Bureau (CFPB) developed a Financial Well-being Scale, which helps assess a person's perceptions about their financial well-being" (FLEC, 2019).

In addition, recognizing the connection to student outcomes, Centers for Teaching Excellence at colleges and universities, charged with the mission to provide professional development, address pedagogical best practices as well as strategies to manage student needs that might look at collaboration across various services areas within the college.

Focusing on why, as Simon Sinek, denotes in his book *Start with Why*, couldn't be a better prelude for any institution seeking to address and resolve problems particularly when their future depends on it. And for higher education, its future does. More importantly, even if the answer to the why is clear and a path reveals itself, the realization evident is that change may only happen when all essential players understand the why and believe in the role they will play. Herein lies the greatest challenge, as analysts, influencers, strategists, and action-oriented individuals come together to plan improvements.

Understanding the who, the what, and the how about students is a critical component of examining and supporting student success. To do so, ongoing communication with the students and gathering of student data can begin to paint a picture.

One example is Mercer County Community College (MCCC), one of nineteen community colleges in the state of New Jersey, which embarked on a scalable restructuring of its student services organization to that aim. A work-in-progress, MCCC has been active in sharing its unfolding model with all who seek to better serve and advance student success. While serving its student body, the strategies behind the model employed at this institution are tool-agnostic, which makes it relevant for others to consider how they might repurpose strategies.

As MCCC has progressed through the transformation, so have sister and partner institutions mobilizing in a collaborative manner. The New Jersey Center for Student Success, which has been providing guidance and resources to the state's nineteen community colleges to establish pathways to improve advising and student success can attest to the work in motion. Workshops emphasizing the need to redesign advising with the guidance of leading experts in the field of education have been a focal point for the Center for Student Success to help institutions address this critical need inarguably affecting student success rates.

At MCCC the process began with an idea that would address the gap in services while maximizing internal resources so as not to add undue burden to the college. The expectation to strengthen customer service and provide students with expanded and convenient advising support services that would positively impact enrollment and retention was exciting. However, the changes met with some hesitation and apprehension. At a time when the college's strategic plan had been refined listing ensuring student success as its first goal, misgivings about the new structure that would buttress this goal took precedence, but a core group of individuals gradually began to share the vision, implement the plan, and begin the disruptive and timely innovations that would unfold.

A work-in-progress, this process has required the willingness, participation, and expertise of many. All areas of the college are critically involved and soliciting their support, ideas, and contributions is essential, not a one-shot deal.

Dr. Charlie L. Nutt, NACADA executive director, underscores that educators should recognize holistic advising is an institution-wide effort, "just not academic affairs, or student affairs." It is really building a campus-wide approach to student success initiatives. He explains how many campuses have a multitude of initiatives going on across the campus that may be duplicative—"all may be hitting the same group of students but no one is really aware of what the other side is doing." The NACADA organization came into existence as a result of the first National Conference on Academic Advising in 1977. Notable in academic advising conversations and its evolution, NACADA has a membership exceeding 10,000 across the United States, Puerto Rico, Canada, and internationally.[2]

Dr. Nutt says institutions should have an institutional plan that clearly outlines what is happening in student affairs, academic affairs, with advising, tutoring, and other areas of the college. Also communication should be coordinated so students are not barraged with emails. For example, avoid "one group of students getting 40 emails a week about all the services that are available to the point that they just want to walk away because they are just tired of being told that they need help," he says. Messages should be vetted and streamlined so students are all receiving the information they need, and one group of students is not getting too much attention while others are omitted, "because we are assuming they are doing fine because they don't meet the predictive analytics that your database shows."

As for approaches to support student success, Dr. Gates Black, president of Delaware County Community College, shares:

> Ideally the best way is to not do away with a face-to-face interaction, infusing tech where appropriate and understanding the access that they have. The college has to become more focused. There was a time when college was a cafeteria model . . . and students can be overwhelmed by too many choices. (reference to a catalog listing degree and program offerings). Creating centers of excellence is a possibility through which colleges . . . might be able to hone in on specific areas but for that to happen there has to be compromise. So how do we work together to create a center of excellence around particular items.

A guiding question institutions should ask themselves is: what actions or changes will really help students. Dr. Gates Black suggests that if an institution is prepared to ask the question, then "that means that we have to be ready to change when necessary. It's about becoming a student-ready college."

This raises the issue of how schools use data, early alerts, and predictive analytics. In addition to examining student assessment data, institutions should determine what communication to share with all students, even those students who are not flagged. Communication can serve to remind, warn, inquire, extend help, as well as reward. And this type of interaction helps institutions build relationships with their students.

At institutions that have experienced success and continue to move the needle to improve retention, the first step is to look at the service holistically and the flow of service. Understanding the nature of their students and the importance of enhancing communication and support services as a priority, during Dr. Donald Generals' first year as president of Community College of Philadelphia (CCP), he was able to increase the college's advising team to more than a dozen.

While these service points and resources also existed, at MCCC for example, leaders recognized a disconnect on campus that would eclipse the dedicated efforts of many. This new passage would embolden and multiply those wholehearted intentions and provide the college with a strong foundation that would maintain and sustain continuity of services to students to successfully guide them through their college experience.

Assessment and reassessment is key when institutions are faced with the proverbial question: how are we doing? A first step is revisiting what the institution thinks it already understands: student demographics. Next, a review of the tools currently being used to determine their value, level of use, followed by identifying if new tools would be needed and the practicality of doing so. Communication is another area of importance that requires some attention. Questions to posit are as follows:

- How is internal and external information communicated?
- What does student outreach look like?
- How are important student messages communicated to students and how can receipt be confirmed?
- Where are the disconnects in the communication process?
- How many students receive advising services?
- How long are those sessions? What do those sessions entail?
- Who advises students?
- Where do students go for help—advising or otherwise?

Thanks to innovative thinking and partnerships, higher education has been finding ways to curb and reverse declining enrollments. Although it may still be too early to say if community colleges and four-year institutions have turned the corner, enrollments at some colleges are holding steady and others are showing promising signs. Despite some upticks, college leaders realize that gone are the golden days of enrollment, when high FTEs were the standard: "Enrollment in both the public two-year sector and the for-profit sector of postsecondary education increased rapidly between 2000 and 2010, but it has declined since then."[3]

The other elephant in the room is declining state funding in community colleges, which has also put a strain the survival of these institutions. According to the Center on Budget and Policy Priorities:

> overall state funding for public two- and four-year colleges in the 2017 school year (that is, the school year ending in 2017) was nearly $9 billion below its 2008 level, after adjusting for inflation . . . The funding decline has contributed to higher tuition and reduced quality on campuses as colleges have had to balance budgets by reducing faculty, limiting course offerings, and in some cases closing campuses.

In many cases, these cuts have resulted in consolidation of community colleges and mergers between two-year and four-year institutions. While the cost savings are evident, the positive impact on student services is anticipated but remains to be seen. New Jersey was not absolved from these cuts, and in some counties such as Mercer County, local support and innovation have and are making a difference. Steady county funding coupled with innovative leadership has buttressed many of the changes designed at MCCC that have revamped advising and student support.

Nationwide, while colleges are feeling the consequences of low enrollments, many have found lessons with the harsh experiences served by this declining trend. Motivated by necessity and the will to preserve enrollments and attract new students, colleges like MCCC, for example, which in 2016 made a bold move to revise its advising structure, are reassessing, retooling, and moving forward. Elements that were formerly part of Student Services would find a home under the wing of Academic Affairs in a new division that would oversee academically related student services to provide a systematic, cohesive, and comprehensive approach to resources students need to be successful.

Anthony Carnevale, director of the Center on Education and the Workforce at Georgetown University, is quoted in "Community College Enrollment Drops", a 2016 *Inside Higher Ed* article as saying that while typically people go to college with the expectation of advancing their career at some point, the cost of going to college seems to outweigh the benefits for some: "Nobody can see clearly how to use the postsecondary system to get a job. It's confusing, cumbersome and it's expensive." This provocative comment is a key motivator for institutions to update how they provide education, which ultimately can contribute to retention, completion, and greater enrollment.

To that end institutions like the John N. Gardner Institute for Excellence in Undergraduate Education, NACADA, and the New Jersey Council of

Community Colleges' Center for Student Success are committed to provide higher education with a toolkit to address advising, which is at the core of the student experience. In *Inside Higher Ed*, Drew Koch, president and chief operating officer of the Gardner Institute, who together with NACADA led a two-year national initiative to help a cohort of colleges and universities redesign academic advising, submits that there "are scores of vendors who sell technology solutions for academic advising . . . they do very little to change the actual processes, practices and culture associated with academic advising at a college or university—at least not in any intentional way." The Excellence in Academic Advising Project, by contrast, is "something completely missing on the higher education landscape today—and the absence of a process like this may shed light on why many advising 'solutions' do not quite yield their desired results," notes Koch in the article entitled "Initiative Seeks to Overhaul Academic Advising."

Adding new tools isn't exactly the answer to everything. At MCCC there were many tools, but the questions asked were—were the tools fully integrated, fully functional, were they purposeful, and the folks who needed to use them—did they? The other questions dealt with appropriate access and training.

Kevin Gannon delivers a salient point in an opinion piece published in the *Chronicle of Higher Education*, as he recognizes solutions and initiatives aimed at increasing enrollment and student persistence: "partnerships with local secondary schools, summer bridge programs, First-Year Experience programs, new student seminars built around a college success curriculum, expansion of developmental coursework, a stronger focus on diversity in student services and campus life." Gannon, however, notes that "persistence and completion rates are tied to enrollments, and working on the former offers a promising way forward in maintaining the latter. In short, if you can't recruit additional students, you need to make every effort to keep more of the ones you already have." Not coincidentally, this is exactly the state of higher education yesterday, today, and in the near future.

Using strategies and campaigns that were successful in the past are not necessarily fruitful in meeting current challenges despite a past relatively successful track record. In seeking current solutions, there is benefit from tapping into what worked previously by making some adjustments or recognizing that times have changed and a different perspective may be more workable. Every effort counts.

To Gannon's point about inclusive teaching, it is an important strategy that can complement other support efforts to provide students with positive experiences that will help them persist. According to Cornell University's Center for Teaching Innovation, inclusive teaching incorporates universal design, embedded diversity, as well as active learning and teaching strategies that can provide students with feelings of connectedness and increase their levels of comfortability. This mindset aligns with the inclusive and intrusive practices that were adopted to take the student satisfaction challenge by the horns and revision advising services at MCCC. Similarly, other campuses around the country are forming their own.

Leadership at institutions such as Community College of Philadelphia in Pennsylvania, and Rockland Community College, and Stella and Charles Guttman Community College (Guttman Community College) in New York (which has a robust advising and peer mentoring model) demonstrates an understanding that an holistic approach advances the pursuit of student success. At MCCC, the strategic planning goal to ensure student success takes a holistic and targeted approach by identifying student cohorts in order to improve outreach communication and intrusive advising. By doing so, no student is left behind, in the sense that proactive efforts are made to share relevant information and resources, and provide access to all without waiting for students to walk in.

In the mission to support student success, which correlates highly to the community surrounding the institution, of critical importance is an ongoing commitment to developing the college team and being willing to take guidance regardless of rank or title. Dr. Gates Black shares, while recalling a mentor, that no matter how much one knows, the approach is that you can still continue to learn. "There is a humbleness that comes with that. It's an asset."

Rockland Community College has over 7,000 students and its president, Dr. Michael A. Baston, speaks to the model that works for them:

> We have a holistic student support model through what we call a student support team. Each student has a dean for the school they are assigned to, the program director connected to their academic program, a connection counselor that provides mental health and other wrap around support services. They have a dedicated financial aid person, a dedicated career and academic advisor, which is sort of their success counselor who helps to really coordinate all the support services for the student. And students when they come in they are given an assessment to help them explore what their potential opportunities are as well as for us to understand what other wrap around support services they might need when they enroll.

Dr. Baston notes that information collected becomes a part of the work that they do in the college's connections center. "Our connections center basically has direct connections with United Way, and with other community-based organizations. That is a very intentionally focused infrastructure. Clearly, we have a robust approach here."

Coordinated and individual efforts complement and support the holistic approach to connecting with and serving students. At Rider University, Lawrenceville, New Jersey, Dr. Sharon Sherman, faculty and former dean of Education, says, "I make personal calls to students on a regular basis to simply ask, 'How is everything going?' If necessary, resources are provided. Students follow up with me so I know they're on track to achieve success." According to its Facts & Figures, Rider University has 3,900 undergraduate and 927 graduate students representing 63 countries, 39 states, and 2 U.S. territories. It also offers 71 undergraduate and 28 graduate degree programs in business administration, education, liberal arts, sciences, music, fine and performing arts, counseling, human services and leadership, and 27 undergraduate and graduate certifications.[4]

Courtney Brazile, faculty, Mountain View College, an open-access public community college that is one of seven separately accredited colleges of the Dallas County Community College District in Texas, says, "I coordinate campus programs that allow students to become involved in their institution beyond the four walls of the classroom."

Dr. Sheila Perkins, educator and authentic facilitator and coach, has been involved in higher education and conducting corporate, community, and various other industry training for over 15 years. She also has taught in online formats for 12 years. In thinking about how best to support student success and afford a sense of community and belonging to students, Dr. Perkins shares:

> I began to reflect on student success outcomes in my classes and asked myself, too, how do I get success started? First, it is essential for me to establish a class-culture that will favor and embrace content. It is important to create an environment of community, so that learners feel energized and comfortable to process content more deeply. To help with processing, at the beginning of all sessions, I announce that all conversations are confidential; that each assembly will be a safe place to discuss, and share information. I use first-sessions to get-to-know all learners through introductions—mine included—and then pose 3–4 questions each person is to answer. Trust building starts, and usually over a short span of time—even if I am conducting a one-day session—connection is established, quickly. I believe that there is tremendous power in connection. Learners begin to engage with one another and with me, comfortably. On-going engagement becomes easier when learners feel included in the learning process. (I use humor and stories as well, to forge relationships with students.) The more I know, and understand about learners, the more I can develop motivating lesson plans—which include various modalities—and this equates to more energized learners, and student success.

How to face the challenge of declining enrollments is a bear, but adopting inclusive and intrusive advising practices assists in sustaining current enrollments so students who are facing challenges of their own don't discontinue their education. Data from the National Student Clearinghouse Research show that persistence is more pronounced in certain student cohorts, which supports strategies that differentiate student demographics.

CUSTOMER OR STUDENT SATISFACTION

With enrollment decline looming at campuses nationwide, initiatives, conversations, workshops, strategic plans, and more at institutions center on how to tackle and reverse this consequence. In serving while preserving existing enrollment and aiming to secure more students, questions about student satisfaction arise. What exactly does that mean and how does it translate to enrollment, retention, completion, and student success?

Depending on who is involved in the discussion, students are considered customers and therefore customer satisfaction is critical in advancing student success. Others agree about serving students well to achieve the same end but the approach is said to be student-centric not customer-focused. Semantics? Are they both saying the same thing? Question of value or is it rather a question of fact?

These are important inquiries; however, it is relevant to note that stakeholders may not all see eye-to-eye, except for the end in mind, which is how the journey toward ensuring student success begins. No matter which term is selected or perspective embraced, the lens through which student success is viewed illustrates individuals who are fulfilled. Fulfillment can be translated into how the students' goals are articulated. That can mean transfer to another institution to complete a four-year degree, internship experiences during the college journey, or professional development for some learners, all with the ultimate goal of improving one's competitiveness, marketability, and employability.

But can an institution determine its potential success rate by the instructional, advising, or coaching models adopted? Probably as much as educators could argue about the success of varying pedagogical practices from lecture-based to those that expect students to be more active in their own learning such as flipped, problem-based, or discovery-based models. While students have so much to gain from student-centered teaching and learning methods that allow them to curate and explore and take the lead in what and how they learn, the role of the faculty is not diminished and is critical in providing guidance and support.

In a 2015 piece published in Slate, Rebecca Schuman justifies the belief that students are not customers: "By the very nature of what they are signing up to do, college students are *not* always right, and since customers *are* always right . . . well, you know how a syllogism works. Thus the nonprofit university should not be acting like a corporation." The notion that students or customers are not always right is recognized by higher institutions regardless of their perspective toward students since central to the mission of learning institutions is to afford guidance and education, which sets the tone for the student-institutional relationship, tilting a bit away from the customer-business model.

Similarly in 2015, Patrick McGhee noted in The Guardian and a year later in a TEDx Talks: TEDx University of Bolton how he also believes students should just be students and not commodities. McGhee argues:

> Seeing students as customers in the traditional sense narrows our perceptions of them, the potential for their relationship with their university and the kind of help from which they would benefit. A student who struggles to engage isn't a business problem but a human being who perhaps needs someone to talk to, and to listen. This is critical and points to how the holistic nature of service provided to students is or should be a guiding principle in higher education.

It follows that businesses are of the mindset that in order for colleges to sustain and grow enrollments, student satisfaction is at the core and therefore the concept that students are like customers and should be advocated as a viable solution. This is gospel to organizations such as Destiny Solutions, an enterprise software company that focuses on the nontraditional education market, whose mantra reads: "We only succeed when our customers succeed." On its website, its mantra is followed by the explanation: "It's this fundamental belief that defines us, guides us, and drives us to ensure that each school we partner with achieves their strategic goals."

In a 2016 interview in the *EvoLLLution*, a Destiny Solutions publication, Bea González, vice president for Community Engagement, Syracuse University, supports the customer service mindset toward students:

> If you're concerned about the student experience at your institution then yes, you need to focus on customer service. Leaders are interested in these things because, as we all know, millennials are changing the way we do business. They're looking for quicker answers, they're looking for answers in places that we never thought people would. . . . Whether we call it customer service, excellence in teaching, or the student experience, it's all about putting the learner at the center of operations.

Irrespective of student or customer, recognizing students' end in mind proves to be more effective in sustaining institutional goals while meeting student needs and providing them with a toolkit that will embolden them as they move along their education paths. In addition, having a firm grasp of the student demographic and its transitory nature given current trends, socioeconomic, and market factors are critical in serving students.

AGILITY OF TECHNOLOGY

Building something for the many, not the few, is not an easy task, but critically important to be nimble. Purposeful use of technology can support the need for this flexibility to make adjustments as student cohorts change and expand. In the case of MCCC, the college pursued a technology-mediated student success model that enhanced the college's ability to connect with the student body, enhance multimodal education and experiential opportunities, develop dynamic advising structures to address ever-changing student needs, and anticipate future trends.

Lessons learned showcase how the use of the learning management system also affords productive and innovative collaborations to enhance online education, retention, completion, and ultimately student success. Also, Advisor Trac and Tutor Trac,[5] tools that facilitate tracking student visits with advisors and learning center sessions, helped sustain the advising model.

Moreover, for ease of navigation in higher education, the use of mobile compatible tools, which embody a one-stop or no-stop mindset for information and services, is recommended. MCCC's organizational structure encouraged and provided cross-functional communication and supported campus-wide as well as technology integration, ongoing assessment, and data-driven strategies to make student success everyone's business, as repeatedly noted by Dr. Jianping Wang, president of Mercer County Community College (MCCC).

Equally important is the practice of aligning institutional strategic plans with student success, such as developing innovative partnerships, ensuring that students accomplish their academic and career goals, and investing in organizational and professional effectiveness. An example of this is Manypathsonefuture.org, whose ambition goal "to raise the percentage of New Jersey residents who have attained an industry-valued credential or college degree from the current 50 percent up to 65 percent by 2025" can be made possible with the help of many key players in education and business who can join to increase and strengthen innovative partnerships between these two groups, as well as expand college transfer and career awareness. Success coaches, for example, armed with this type of knowledge and access to trending information can be instrumental in building clearer pathways for students.

Also, the changes that illustrate cross-functional teams at an institution support goals to enrich academic and career planning and advisement opportunities. In the 2014 Gallup-Purdue index report Brandon Busteed, executive director of Gallup Education and Workforce Development, advocates these types of relationships particularly for careers exploration. According to the 2014 Gallup-Purdue index report, alumni who identified as having "had a mentor who encouraged me to pursue my goals and dreams" were more likely to agree that their education was worth the cost. The report also highlights that "supportive and motivating relationships with professors and mentors are crucial to undergraduates' college experience."

The 2016 Survey of Entering Student Engagement (SENSE) results reveal need to improve in areas concerning advising, for example, the number of times entering students were required to participate in an academic advising session, whether an academic advisor was provided with additional resources concerning support services, and discussed or planned a follow-up advising session. Similarly, the 2016 Community College Survey of Student Engagement results suggest that the college should also take note of factors that might preclude students from scheduling courses and increase noncognitive support services that help students cope with life issues, including family, time management, and work.

A companion survey to the Community College Survey of Student Engagement is the Community College Faculty Survey of Student Engagement (CCFSSE), which found in 2016 that both full-time and part-time faculty do not refer students to academic support services as often as they could. All these findings point to a need to augment and reinforce cross-functional communication and advising services.

A webinar presented on October 26, 2017, entitled Recruiting, Engaging and Retaining Generation Z students (born after 1996), revealed how this group of individuals has been found to be "the most anxious generation to arrive on campus." Barry Telford, CEO, Universities West Sodexo North America, which partners with clients to provide quality-of-life services, explained during the University Business Web Seminar. The 2017 results of their survey, which "polled more than 1,000 students and 4,000 globally about their expectations, concerns, values" regarding higher education. The research found how Generation Z students are "looking for immediate reaction, which is contributing to an increased stress level . . . and motivating many universities and their partners to consider a whole new model of service" that supports their desire for community, a sense of belonging, and a concern about their future, said Telford.

Time and again, the idea of relationship-building comes to the surface and echoes the realization that authentic connections that support continuity of service and access to resources provide a stronger advising pathway which leads to enrollment, retention, and completion—three top higher education priorities. Self-service academic planning tools such as Ellucian Colleague Student Planning, advisement and tutoring tracking tools, early alert systems in higher education, and the use of learning management systems make more of this possible.

Expanding advising circles, with the addition of success coaches and mentors to complement faculty advisors, can contribute to growing formal and informal connections that can help student thrive. In a 2018 article in the *Chronicle of Higher Education*, "Relationships are Central to the College Experience: Can colleges engineer them?," that discusses the important role mentorships can play in a student's life, Beckie Supiano writes that "colleges can create conditions that make relationships more likely to form." These relationships assist students navigate academic, personal, and professional college scenarios, which could challenge their success. "Long after they have forgotten much of the content learned in class, alumni maintain connections with friends, teachers." While there is no magic calculation to build and sustain this critical connection between students and institutions, it is that spark that will keep higher education doors open and its students on track to completion and beyond.

According to University Business' *Outlook 2018*, "Student services—a key piece of the success puzzle—are getting more attention; 60 percent of respondents say services will be greater priority this year than in 2017. Areas getting most renewed attention since 2018 are admissions and academic help/retention." Survey results of top overall priorities of campus leaders list student success initiatives at the top (86%). And so here it is.

NOTES

1. Hyman, C. L. (2018). *Reinvention: the Promise and Challenge of Transforming A Community College System*. Harvard Education Press, Cambridge, MA.

2. NACADA. (n.d.). The History of NACADA Updated 2006. Retrieved from https://nacada.ksu.edu/About-Us/History.aspx.

3. College Board. (2016, April). Trends in Community College Enrollment. Retrieved from https://trends.collegeboard.org/sites/default/files/trends-in-community-colleges-research-brief.pdf.

4. Rider University, (n.d.). Facts & Figures. https://www.rider.edu/about-rider/facts-figures.

5. Trac Systems by Redrock Software Corporation. Retrieved from https://www.go-redrock.com/products/tutortrac/#:~:text=TutorTrac%20is%20the%20complete%20management,support%20students%20in%20higher%20education.

Chapter 2

Assessing Enrollment Realities

So what can be learned from case studies of institutions that have experienced some level of success? Why should dissimilar institutions from disparate geographical locations, with varying student demographics, listen closely to higher-ed colleagues? What can be gained from walking through their pathways? The answer is: a whole lot. Despite differences, there is as much common ground in the challenges and agnostic strategies that can give insight to what higher education can do to support student success.

What this all means is accepting the positive in change as a constant and embracing a new normal. This converging realization has been the focus of the higher education narrative that has inspired conversations, discussions, collaborations, debates, unrest, and sleepless nights as institutions assess and address the realities facing most.

With few exceptions, the current reality is that enrollment is not what it used to be. But as demonstrated by education new accounts and in the book *Becoming a Student-Ready College*, by Tia Brown McNair, Susan Albertine, Michelle Asha Cooper, Nicole McDonald, and Thomas Major, Jr., the solution can be found within each institution by being open to assessing their realities and developing workable solutions that in some cases might entail change. Actually, change is inevitable. Change does not exactly mean out with the old and in with the new; it can simply be a mindset adjustment. Yes, again change; change can take the form of interdepartmental collaborations, policy synthesizing, communication, resource sharing, and cross-functional training, where you maintain experts but also expand on generalists for support. According to *Becoming a Student-Ready College*, "the motivation needs to flow from heartfelt commitment to the human, faith-based, or civic responsibility of the institution . . . people . . . have to care about making change" (p. 57).

A concern that affects retention can be summed up with one letter: *F*. Failure can be attributed to many factors, but ultimately it translates into students exhausting financial awards due to a lack of guided pathway, switching majors, course repetition In the *Chronicle Review*, Bill Conley (2019) commented that "yield models had been invalidated by a sea change in student college-choice behavior." This sea change encompasses much more. It represents multifarious factors, including food insecurities, student demographics, minimum wage, job opportunities, financial obligations, and inaccessibility, that have also disrupted pre-semester highs and customary lows to ride the tide of expectations that enrollment would line up as it had in the past. While some institutions are faring better than others, overall, the National Student Clearinghouse Research Center reported a decrease in U.S. college enrollment "for the eighth consecutive year" (Hain, 2019). Ongoing data trends discussions sound the alarm that compel institutions to revision how they can continue to serve as conduits to student success. The goal is to be open to self-inquiry in order to begin to identify the issues, find solutions, and address change.

In seeking solutions that will help institutions guide students toward success, understanding what student success means to students is an important factor. To that end, in fall 2018, the Community College Libraries and Academic Support for Student Success (CCLASSS) project surveyed 10,844 students across seven community colleges to explore student needs from the student perspective to strengthen library services and help to bridge curricular to noncurricular student needs. A multiyear initiative, the CCLASSS project was led by Northern Virginia Community College and Ithaka S+R. The Institute of Museum and Library Services (IMLS), four community colleges from different New York City boroughs, and three community colleges from New York State, Virginia, and Washington were represented. In the study, students weighed in on key concepts or characteristics of support, particularly Knowledge Base and Personal Librarian. This supports the idea that not all students are the same nor they have the same challenges or needs.

Forty-four percent of student respondents deemed Knowledge Base as extremely valuable noting: Imagine that the college offered a single point of contact for whenever you need help navigating any part of college, including advising, registering for classes, applying for financial aid, securing personal counseling, and obtaining tutoring or other coursework assistance. This service would offer expertise in connecting you with the right college employee for assistance.[1]

Throughout her tenure, Dr. Jianping Wang, president of Mercer County Community College, New Jersey, has sought ways to improve, extend, and expand student success. Aspirational goals, communication, and decisions made with the student in mind have been a constant for this institution. "The essence is still innovation—not to be content with what we have tried before;

in our assessment determine what has worked or not worked. The goal is to really understand our student needs. This generation of learners are so diverse and their needs vary."

The use of success coaches as a point of contact has provided continuity and a sense of community for students. Recognizing and embracing the diversity of its student population, Dr. Wang acknowledges that for Mercer a one-size-fits-all model does not achieve results. "Students come in all sizes, shapes, and have varying needs and expectations." To ensure student success, colleges need to recognize, respect, and respond to those student challenges and not "just pay lip service," says Dr. Wang. Actions must be mindful, concrete, and deliberate. "If you don't innovate, you become stagnant, left behind and irrelevant. Innovation is the name of the game," she continues.

STRATEGIES AT CCP

Dr. Donald Generals, president of Community College of Philadelphia, notes: "community colleges, especially, have emulated the four-year institutions, which are very traditional, they have very ensconced hierarchical structures—prereqs, co-requisites, developmental education and everything in between. And I think the nature of student needs warrants a level of flexibility that you are able to customize, at least their academic needs in a way that is beneficial to them as opposed to being consistent with the traditions, policies and structures of the institution."

While the college recognizes the value of concurrent enrollment, the Accelerated Learning Program (ALP) method, online, virtual, distributed education models, Generals adds, "they are extremely difficult to implement when you have ossified approaches and philosophies toward education in the institution, which can be a struggle." However, as a Guided Pathways institution, Dr. Generals shares how that has moved CCP forward; one factor is having targeted conversations with students from day one:

> Operationally as a president you have to see how the entire enterprise is connected to what [you] want to do as it relates to facilitating student success. I know pathways [is] just one word but redesigning your institution in such a way that you have curriculum alignment, you do away with superfluous curriculum. You look at ways to align the developmental ed programing with the programs that students go into. You assign your student services to particular programs so they are not random. Reorganizing the institution around this pathway model is really designed to get students thinking about and executing a plan for being successful from the first day they come into the college.

Embracing a positive or growth-minded approach rather than a deficit model can also be beneficial. In 2018, Mike Colagrossi published in Big

Think: "10 reasons why Finland's education system is the best": "Finland's educational system doesn't worry about artificial or arbitrary merit-based systems. There are no lists of top performing schools or teachers. It's not an environment of competition—instead, cooperation is the norm." While the article looks at Finland's entire education system, and this book is focusing on higher education, the idea of extending the student-faculty rapport makes sense as the connection and the mentor that emerge can lead to student success. "Students in Finland often have the same teacher for up to six years of their education. During this time, the teacher can take on the role of a mentor or even a family member. During those years, mutual trust and bonding are built so that both parties know and respect each other," notes Colagrossi.

How to address the needs of students in order to retain them and guide them toward success requires institutions to consider strategies that work outside their immediate sphere of influence and zone of comfortability. In a documentary, Randi Weingarten, president of the American Federation of Teachers, observed on a tour in Finland the country's educational mindset and stated, "People are engaged in problem solving, the notion that someone is an obstacle is irrelevant. The conversation is how can we all together work to help children."

This is idea can be expanded to higher education. Instead of focusing on student deficiencies, why not look to identify what institutions can do to address student needs and challenges. In this vein, institutions can also observe how inequalities of any kind can impact student success. Finnish educator, professor of Education Policy and Deputy Director of the Gonski Institute at the University of New South Wales in Sydney, Australia. and author of *Finnish Lessons: What Can the World Learn from Educational Change in Finland*, Pasi Sahlberg, noted this correlation, explaining how the countries with the greatest income distribution inequality tend to demonstrate lower learning outcomes.

Revisioning how existing tools and technologies are employed is another way of addressing challenges. (1) Looking at institutional data as a means to identify areas that need support or triage. (2) If graduation rates need improvement, for example, then paying attention to student demographics and tailoring programs for those populations to maximize successful completion. (3) Realizing that it's okay to do things a little differently or a lot differently depending on the situation. (4) Understanding that there is no ego in an entrenched plan that no longer works. Why hold on to things that no longer yield results? Equally important is understanding that fixation on holding on to a past that has run its course is not the way to build or honor legacy of experiences that contributed to the foundation of an institution's success. Change may be difficult to embrace but this is not new to higher education.

In "The Student Personnel Point of View" (1949), it is evident this conversation dates back to an holistic approach and the awareness that institutions needed to adapt: "The student personnel point of view encompasses the student as a whole. The concept of education is broadened to include attention to the student's well-rounded development physically, socially, emotionally and spiritually, as well as intellectually. The student is thought of as a responsible participant in his own development and not as a passive recipient of an imprinted economic, political, or religious doctrine, or vocational skill."

Despite generational pains and arguments on either side, colleges continue to work diligently to demonstrate that institutions of higher learning will continue to be relevant. Mercer County Community College's president, Dr. Wang states:

> The education experience we provide to students has to provide affordable, accessible, relevant education to their future careers, employability. The skills they learn from us can be easily utilized in their professional careers. We have been criticized by a lot of employers that students get into a lot of debt and can't get a job. Also from employers, they state 'I pay a lot of money to someone with a degree, but they don't have what I need them to know.' The idea that we don't produce students who are ready to work for them. That is a pretty serious indictment of what we do as education institutions. In the old days people hired based on credentials . . . B.A, M.A., PhD; today they say that with less certainty that those credentials signify those employees are ready to work.

Regarding the value of legacy, also critical is to face what worked, and extracting from successful ideas, teams, process, implementation, or strategy the nuggets that can motivate or inspire change to address the current challenge. Distilling solutions from prior knowledge and new knowledge is the key. Paraphrased, a colleague once iterated the importance of humility to accept not always having the answers, but understanding the importance and being willing to follow the lead others have set.

NOTE

1. Blankstein, Melissa, Christine Wolff-Eisenberg, and Braddlee. "Student Needs Are Academic Needs: Community College Libraries and Academic Support for Student Success." Ithaka S+R. Last Modified September 30, 2019. https://doi.org/10.18665/sr.311913.

Chapter 3

Financial Mindset for Student Success

In assessing realities, which entails evaluation of resource allocation, uses, and distribution, knowledge of the college's financial health and communication between senior leadership, administrators, faculty, and college finance officers should not be underestimated. Similarly, financial literacy and wellness are the other side of the coin and form part of the holistic services toolkit to help students. As part of this financial literacy endeavor, the Financial Literacy and Education Commission (FLEC) (2019) also recommends that institutions advise students on loans, majors, and obstacles to graduation, and make available emergency aid to help bridge gaps between financial aid and the resources students need to complete their education.[1] Financial wellness or literacy is a means to help students learn about how to make sound financial choices. "Critical decisions that students and families make before, during, and after their postsecondary education influence their financial future," (FLEC, 2019) In the same vein, staff, faculty, and administrators should be able have those same resources at their disposal.

Published in the *U.S. Financial Literacy and Education Commission's Best Practices for Financial Literacy and Education at Institutions of Higher Education* are recommendations that suggest enhancing this support by embracing an approach that parallels and complements advising and coaching practices such as:

- providing clear, timely, and customized information to inform student borrowing, and
- targeting different student populations by use of national, institutional, and individual data.

Timely targeted communication, ongoing support, student engagement, and a focus on next steps and life after graduation undergird this. From the Consumer Financial Protection Bureau's *Five Principles of Effective Financial Education* key principles recommended for adoption are as follows:

- Know the individuals and families to be served.
- Financial education, information, and delivery methods must be tailored to the circumstances and needs of the user.[2]

"The more the path is designed to help a person make and follow-through on choices that help her meet her goals, the less that person may need know-how and motivation to get to the same place."[3]

Given this focus, it raises the question, how much of this information is consumed by administrators who oversee department budgets and make decisions that impact how student support services are executed, supported, and sustained. As there is no evidence that federal, state, and local funding for higher education will be trending up any time in the near future, internal financial literacy is an option that could give institutions staying power and reduce the despondent resolve that raising tuition, attrition, or workforce reductions are the only way.

Facilitating seminars between business officers and administrators responsible for budgets can make a difference in increasing levels of understanding about internal and external higher education financing and financial wellness. The goal of these sessions would be to give administrators a macro- and micro-level view of the budget so they may have a better understanding of the college's financial health, and why certain recommendations or changes are being moved forward. Informed decision-making derives from direct knowledge of the state of the budget and a clearer understanding of financial speak or language:

- unrestricted revenue (tuition and fees, etc.),
- direct and indirect costs (direct labor, direct materials, commissions, piece rate wages, and manufacturing supplies. Examples of indirect costs are production supervision salaries, quality control costs, insurance, and depreciation),
- reimbursable expenses,
- fixed assets (equipment),
- capital versus operating[4] expenditures,
- intangible assets (customer lists, software, brand recognition copyrights, etc.),[5] and
- fringe benefits: "Common examples of fringe benefits include medical and dental insurance, use of a company car, housing allowance, educational assistance, vacation pay, sick pay, meals and employee discounts."[6]

In addition to understanding the language, it is important to understand how the budget is structured. According to "The Flexible Budget:"

"Flexibility usually is structured according to the portion of the budget to which it pertains. Compensation costs account for as much as 60 to 70 percent of most college or university budgets; fixed expenses such as utilities and physical plant maintenance represent approximately 10 to 15 percent. The balance usually is spent for operating expenses such as service contracts, technology, supplies, communication, noncapital equipment, and travel." (excerpt from a new NACUBO book, *College & University Budgeting: An Introduction for Faculty and Academic Administrators*, Third Edition)

Accepting cuts is a tough pill to swallow. What if the administrators realized the benefits of taking a granular look at their budgets that would give them insight to proactively make recommendations and modifications. So why is this important? Ideally, consider the benefits to the college if administrators were as comprehensively schooled about professional budgets as they might regard their personal finances. The goal is not to turn administrators into chief financial officers (CFOs) but to empower them to better represent the needs of their respective areas, supported with a thoughtful and sustainable rationale to the leadership that will have the ultimate say. And for CFOs the message is to consider an information-gathering systems thinking approach that adds more meaning to the budget organizations they oversee. In *A Learning Agenda for Chief Business Officers*, authors recommend financial officers to "consistently gather information and perspectives from a variety of sources. They also share their thinking, so that others can understand how they arrived at their conclusions. This opens the way to honest feedback and the invaluable testing of ideas."[7]

A transparent collaborative planning process that allows for Qs and As is helpful. "Some of the most important budgetary decisions actually occur during the planning process, an essential activity that should precede the budget process and be linked with it. To wield meaningful influence, a participant should be involved in both the planning process and the budget process. The major decisions that influence resource allocations are both process related and content related. For instance, resource allocations are affected just as much by which institutional representatives participate in the process as they are by the actual amount of resources available for allocation."[8]

A LOOK AT ENROLLMENT AND FUNDING

The results published in AACC's *Community College Enrollment Crisis?* reveals that, strikingly, a group showing increased enrollment rates comprises students less than age 18, to 773,000, which can be attributed to dual enrollment or high school students taking credit courses outside of this program (p.5).⁹ However, if institutions do not manage to retain these students to become traditional full-time or part-time undergraduates, the enrollment needle will not officially move, nor will revenue be significantly impacted. "The number of traditional-aged students attending part-time has been a consistent segment of community college enrollment in recent years, while full-time traditional-aged students have been decreasing (down by more than 392,000 students between 2009 and 2017). If this trend continues, part-time students will outnumber full-time students for this age group in the future."¹⁰

During Dr. Generals' first year as president at Community College of Philadelphia (CCP), the advising team expanded to more than a dozen to broaden student support so students could begin having those important conversations about their future. Dr. Generals elaborates:

> So in theory, We want our students to begin talking about where they are going and how they are going to get there . . . basically, executing a plan to be successful from the first day they come into the college. We have organized the institutions into 8 meta majors . . . everything from your developmental ed your first-year experience, your first courses are all vertically aligned, and the advisors and counselors are aligned.

CCP also created a College Promise program, which has been able secure last dollar funding scholarships for about 900 students over the last three years. It's no secret that finances are a critical part of student success. Dr. Generals adds:

> Students drop out because they can't afford it—can't afford books . . . or they drop out because their car got a flat tire . . . the reasons students drop out [are] unbelievable. It can be as small as flat tire or their car broke down. Trying to mitigate that and reduce the number of life circumstances that prevent students from being successful was also part of the goal and continues to be. We have a [long way] to go. We still have enrollment issues, however, our retention numbers are up. Graduation numbers are up. Our overall student satisfaction surveys are up. Our relationship with the community, the business community, city government, is stronger than it was.

With national enrollment at low levels, the stakes are even higher, as increasing tuition could eventually price out students from pursuing an education. Barren classrooms would devastate the livelihoods of educators, the institutions, and more importantly future citizenry. According to AACC's report "Community College Enrollment Crisis?" "the impact on FTE-driven community college funding was even greater than if funding was based on fall headcount enrollment alone."¹¹

According to a GALLUP article, "Using a Strengths-Based Approach to Retain College Students," published by Tom Matson and Jennifer Robinson, "From a student's perspective, dropping out of college can be a ruinous loss of investment and job potential. From a university administration's view, student attrition is financially hazardous in a time of shrinking budgets. For the institution as a whole, every lost student represents lost alumni funding and a mission opportunity for mission fulfillment."[12]

Declining enrollment and education funding are challenging institutions to seek alternative options to stay relevant, given that even tuition increases will no longer seem to be enough. A Pew Charitable Trust issue brief titled, "Two Decades of Change in Federal and State Higher Education Funding" outlines what funding looks like for colleges. Federal funding by level of support comprises:

- Pell Grant and other financial aid,
- research funding,
- veterans education benefits,
- general purpose appropriations (operating expenses for specialized institutions), and
- other federal grant programs (assistance initiatives for disadvantaged students).[13]

"Federal and state funding, together, continue to make up a substantial share of public college and university budgets, at 34 percent of public schools' total revenue in 2017."[14]

In general, state funding (approximately 21%) exceeds federal (13%) contributions but state allotments for elementary and secondary education eclipse that for higher education. In 2017 state category, spending was $78 million for higher education, $283 million for elementary and secondary education.[15]

Options that can translate into cost savings to the institution and ultimately to the student include:

- streamlining software license purchases—individual versus departmental, divisional, or institutional,
- determining the need for organization over individual memberships, travel (attendee versus presenter),
- identifying critical memberships,
- holding revenue generating conferences and events,
- facilitating computer and other equipment purchase versus leasing options,
- expanding open education resources (OER),
- centralizing certain services to avoid duplication,

- making position realignments to meet departmental needs due to service expectations,
- offering pre-retirement packages to reduce broad salary gaps, and
- providing succession planning that aligns with budget forecasts to build the internal pipeline (realizing that it's not just for senior leadership).

LEADERSHIP PROFESSIONAL DEVELOPMENT

Investing in professional development for faculty, staff, and administrators as well as succession planning is crucial to the overall health of the institution and predisposes a mindset toward success. "Frequent unplanned turnover is a problem for the entire institution, and it affects our ability to gain momentum and move forward."[16] The 2019 CUPA-HR Administrators in Higher Education Annual Report noted, "Since the median ages of our presidents, provosts, and deans are 61, 59, and 58, respectively, we must rethink our assumptions about the pathways that lead to these roles. The same is true for other campus VP positions. Looking externally is only going to become more challenging and competitive as these individuals retire or move on." According to the report, "the median age when incumbent 'heads of units' started in the position was 43 and the median age now is 51."

An important factor to consider is the length of time employees have worked in those positions. "The median tenure of leaders in administrative roles is eight years, with very little variance by group. If this sounds familiar, does it mean that there are not sufficient opportunities for advancement at your institution? Does it mean that the individuals in these roles have no interest in higher levels of responsibility? And if leadership positions are revolving doors at your institution, why?"[17]

Approaches that are still worth their value to date include borrowing, partnering, fees, and procurement (Goldstein, 2003). Other strategies can include cost-reduction methods, such as extended financing arrangements, cost-sharing, consortium pricing for goods or services, the use of bonds to finance acquisitions, and outlined multi-year plans to chart technology installations, implementations, and upgrades. Multi-campus or multi-school collaborative shared services approaches or partnerships can offset costs more manageable to partner institutions and expand their capacity (Goldstein, 2003).

While still a challenge, as this can affect bookstore commissions that represent revenue for colleges, open education resources and OER degrees are viable options that reduce the cost of education. This means lower tuition or little to no cost for books to students. OER adoption has certainly expanded in the last decade, although some institutions that have received funding support are further along. In *OER at Scale: The Academic and Economic Outcomes of*

Achieving the Dream's OER Degree Initiative, Dr. Karen A Stout, president and CEO, writes in a letter: "Finally, this work required deep engagement from faculty, who were critical to the initiative's success. It is telling, then, that over the course of the study, participation in the initiative grew to nearly 2,000 faculty. This clearly shows the power of OER as a lever for faculty engagement and is an encouraging sign that these programs will continue to grow."[18]

In the book *The End of College: Creating the Future of Learning and the University of Everywhere*, Kevin Carey sends a foreshadowing message to institutions, faculty, parents, and students, about the inequities and increasingly exorbitant cost of traditional education. He submits how technology has and will continue to serve as a revolutionary transformative force that will change the face of education and make it more accessible. Kindred to OER materials that are digitized, free, and accessible, and what an OER and or an OER degree can mean to students in terms of cost, Carey advances the paradigm shift of brick-and-mortar education to the University of Everywhere. Without the need of a traditional admissions process, "At the University of Everywhere, educational resources that have been scarce and expensive for centuries will be abundant and free. Anything that can be digitized . . . will be available to anyone in the world with in an internet connection" (p. 5).

Carey writes in *The End of* College that what is interesting is the message about reaching students where they are, and meeting students' needs, which is an issue that institutions continue to grapple with, and can give educators pause.

> The personalization will be driven by advances in artificial intelligence and fueled by massive amounts of educational data. Information about student learning will be used to continually adapt and improve people's educational experience based on their unique strengths, needs, flaws and aspiration . . . .Traditional institutions that move quickly and adapt to the opportunities of information technology will become centers of learning in the networked University of Everywhere. Those that cannot change will disappear. (pp. 5, 7)

This type of thinking supports what NACADA and the Gardner Institute have developed in their Excellence in Academic Advising (EAA) initiative, which "addresses these gaps by engaging institutions in a holistic and systemic review of academic advising from a teaching and learning perspective, with support and guidance from experts in the field and experts in educational and organizational change."

NACADA's executive director, Dr. Charlie Nutt adds:

> I think there has to be a real campus-wide incentive for working together toward that. So for example, a self-study of what we are presently doing and we know we

should be doing to reach students, and that everyone on campus is involved with that piece. For that program . . . we have developed 9 conditions of excellence of advising[19] and institutions involved in this project do a 2-year self-study looking at those 9 conditions of excellence for advising, and for each of the conditions, there is a subcommittee that the campus puts together to do an analysis of those 9 conditions. But it has to represent faculty, students, administrators, student service personnel, primary role advisors, students, so that everyone is involved in that analysis of where we need to be and where we need to focus on tearing down those arbitrary brick walls that exist between academic affairs and student affairs and business affairs, understanding that we all must work together.

NOTES

1. U.S. Financial Literacy and Education Commission (2019). Best practices for financial literacy and education at the institutions of higher education. Retrieved from https://home.treasury.gov/system/files/136/Best-Practices-for-Financial-Literacy-and-Education-at-Institutions-of-Higher-Education2019.pdf.

2. U.S. Financial Literacy and Education Commission (2019). Best practices for financial literacy and education at the institutions of higher education. Retrieved from https://home.treasury.gov/system/files/136/Best-Practices-for-Financial-Literacy-and-Education-at-Institutions-of-Higher-Education2019.pdf.

3. Consumer Financial Protection Bureau (2017, June). Effective financial education: Five principles and how to use them. Retrieved from https://s3.amazonaws.com/files.consumerfinance.gov/f/documents/201706_cfpb_five-principles-financial-well-being.pdf.

4. What Are the Differences between Operating and Capital Expenses. Retrieved from https://www.investopedia.com/ask/answers/042415/what-difference-between-operating-expense-and-capital-expense.asp.

5. Intangible Assets. Retrieved from https://www.accountingtools.com/articles/2017/5/12/intangible-asset.

6. Fringe Benefits. Retrieved from https://smallbusiness.chron.com/fringe-benefits-employee-41950.html.

7. A Learning Agenda for Chief Business Officers. Retrieved from http://www.campus-strategies.com/downloads/books_articles/learning_agenda_cbo.pdf.

8. Goldstein, L. (2005, March). College & University Budgeting: An Introduction for Faculty and Academic Administrators, Third Edition. Retrieved from http://www.campus-strategies.com/downloads/books_articles/the_flexible_budget.pdf.

9. American Association of Community Colleges. Community College Enrollment Crisis: Historical Trends in Community College Enrollment. Retrieved from https://www.aacc.nche.edu/wp-content/uploads/2019/08/Crisis-in-Enrollment-2019.pdf.

10. American Association of Community Colleges. Community College Enrollment Crisis: Historical Trends in Community College Enrollment. Retrieved

from https://www.aacc.nche.edu/wp-content/uploads/2019/08/Crisis-in-Enrollment-2019.pdf.

11. American Association of Community Colleges. Community College Enrollment Crisis: Historical Trends in Community College Enrollment. Retrieved from https://www.aacc.nche.edu/wp-content/uploads/2019/08/Crisis-in-Enrollment-2019.pdf.

12. Matson, T., and Robinson, J. (2018, April 5). Using a Strengths-Based Approach to Retain College Students. GALLUP. Retrieved from https://www.gallup.com/workplace/236063/using-strengths-based-approach-retain-college-students.aspx.

13. The Pew Charitable Trusts. (2019, October 15). Two Decades of Change in Federal and State Higher Education Funding. Retrieved from https://www.pewtrusts.org/en/research-and-analysis/issue-briefs/2019/10/two-decades-of-change-in-federal-and-state-higher-education-funding.

14. The Pew Charitable Trusts (2019, October 15). Two Decades of Change in Federal and State Higher Education Funding. Retrieved from https://www.pewtrusts.org/en/research-and-analysis/issue-briefs/2019/10/two-decades-of-change-in-federal-and-state-higher-education-funding.

15. The Pew Charitable Trusts (2019, October 15). Two Decades of Change in Federal and State Higher Education Funding. Retrieved from https://www.pewtrusts.org/en/research-and-analysis/issue-briefs/2019/10/two-decades-of-change-in-federal-and-state-higher-education-funding.

16. Brantley, A. (2019, August 5). A Call to Action Regarding Succession Planning and Sustainability. Retrieved from https://www.higheredtoday.org/2019/08/05/call-action-regarding-succession-planning-sustainability/.

17. Brantley, A. (2019, August 5). A Call to Action Regarding Succession Planning and Sustainability. Retrieved from https://www.higheredtoday.org/2019/08/05/call-action-regarding-succession-planning-sustainability/.

18. OER at Scale: The Academic and Economic Outcomes of Achieving the Dream's OER Degree Initiative. Retrieved from https://www.achievingthedream.org/resource/17993/oer-at-scale-the-academic-and-economic-outcomes-of-achieving-the-dream-s-oer-degree-initiative.

19. NACADA. (n.d.). Nine Condition of Excellence in Academic Advising. Retrieved from https://nacada.ksu.edu/Portals/0/Resources/Excellence%20in%20Academic%20Advising/documents/NineConditionsofExcellence.pdf.

Chapter 4

Retention 4.0
Disruptors, Adapters, Adopters

So what student success initiatives are successful? The ideas that are successful are the ones that meet the needs of the students and address the challenges of current day. Having an understanding of the times and trends and being forward thinking, while mindful of strategies that have worked, are steps in the right direction. College leadership requires not only knowledge but pragmatic risk taken to effect necessary change. But change must have support at all levels or it will fall through the cracks. You have to pick and choose which one is your Waterloo, which one will you not compromise on, says CCP's Dr. Generals. Student-centered institutions know the value of building partnerships as well as relationships with local boards, board of trustees, and political officials, to make compelling arguments to secure resources needed for student success.

Dr. Generals notes:

You have to make sacrifices in terms of resources. Work with your board. It's not a one man operation. It's not just me or the dean or Vice Presidents. You have to get the board on board in terms of resources that you need to acquire. In our case, we had to make significant pitches to the mayor's office and the governor. They are two sources of main revenue providers, and in each case it was all about student success. [It matters] what are you saying in a very specific way that you are going to do differently that's going to outlay goals and objectives relative to metrics that you hope to achieve. And [explain] how is this money going to help you get there.

CCP has also expanded the scope of its programs by adding career and tech programs to its offerings, and an estimated $30 million, 70,000-square-foot career tech center in West Philadelphia. Dr. Generals shares, "Again all of it has to do with student success. Why do we need a career and tech center? Well, a lot of students to find jobs they need training in advanced manufacturing or computer numerical controls . . . we have a pretty good auto tech program now but we can't do diesel, alternative fuel . . . there is a lot we can't do that would enable our students to be successful in this job market—that building will now allow us the opportunity to provide the training for the 21st century."

In comparison to four-year counterparts, community colleges are fairly young at just over half-a-century old. The reality is that while one would think it would be easier for these younger institutions to update and change, community colleges, many that are modeled after four-year institutions, are having difficulty moving away from core traditions. CCP's Dr. Generals says, "At 55, community colleges have no business being in the tradition. There is no one line answer except: moving away from the tradition. In addition, certainly being more focused on the nature and needs of the student as opposed to the traditions and structures of the institution, which is what the tendency is right now."

Consequently, student success for higher education institutions means students are coming back semester after semester, they are doing well academically and on track to graduate. While there is always room for improvement and updates, traditional student services, which provides incredible support to students by way of mentoring, coaching, and advising, is one that still honors the vision and breadth of the roles as articulated in the Student Personnel Point of View (1949):

> The student personnel movement constitutes one of the most important efforts of American educators to treat the college and university students as individuals, rather than as entries in an impersonal roster. . . . The college or university which accepts these broad responsibilities for aiding in the optimum development of the individual in his relations to society will need to evaluate carefully and periodically its curricular offerings, its method of instruction, and all other resources for assisting the individual to reach his personal goals.

RETENTION STRATEGIES

Guided pathways and holistic advising, including financial wellness or literacy, have been instrumental in keeping students on track. Efforts to reinforce financial literacy also help students understand the cost of college and why their choices impact their bottom line. The work of success coaches and counselors involves advising students and guiding them through the course selection process, and offering suggestions about important life skills necessary to more adroitly navigate each semester. Mentorship and building a sense of community are also key components of the student success formula. And how individual schools proceed depends on their level of understanding of their audience, the students.

Early alert systems also provide another means for colleges to address student success. It involves flagging students who are having issues from the beginning. These flags can track attendance, excessive absences, low grades, poor overall performance, conduct issues, and the like. Mainly, as has been the tradition, faculty launch the early alerts which are directed to a system that can provide supports to the student, with the goal of ultimately closing the loop by addressing the alert. With these tools, advisors, faculty, and staff from key areas can start the conversation and recommend or provide the interventions necessary that can move the student forward and out of the precarious academic situation that was the reason behind the flagged alert.

In order to expand usage of these systems, early alerts could be communicated and circulated to the proper channels, automatically, as well as from support areas to faculty as well as the other way around, a shift from the faculty-initiated approach. And why not? The goal is to keep the right people informed so they can act before it's too late for the student. The expanded use of early alert systems by nonfaculty, a concept unconscionable in some spaces, still has not been ruled out as it can be more broadly and systematically used to communicate, help, and even reward students. While not it does not typically take place in the classroom, advising is in some circles considered teaching. According to *Becoming a Student-Ready College*, "All people who work on campus have the capacity to be effective educators" (p. 35).

Given the features afforded by learning management systems (LMS), the opportunity to expand use outside the traditional course delivery function is ever-present. Used as a platform to exchange information and provide targeted messaging to users, the LMS has multiple applications that support teaching.

At many institutions, like Mercer County Community College and Delaware County Community College (DCCC), the use of the LMS has broadened to include communication and engagement of student groups, provide campus-wide or targeted reminders, and serve as a repository, learning community, college navigation, or training space. More recently, DCCC has taken its LMS a step further: to provide prospective students with an accessible introduction to the DCCC student life cycle from enrollment to completion—all they need to know, contact information, plus a peek at the learning management system by way of the LMS platform.

In this manner, the use of technology, caseload or cohort models can be scaled up. Technology-mediated platforms and streamlined messaging via email or text facilitate targeted nudging and can expand communication and access.

Reducing student attrition is often done one student at a time. Small percentage increases can translate into overall enrollment increases. Conducting exit interviews to find out why they want to leave can also help retain students; while inquiring about their reason for withdrawing, students may decide to delay reentry but outline a plan with help, explore and secure resources, so they can continue their education. While it is a student's right to withdraw from a course or decide to take a gap semester, it doesn't hurt to ask why they want to drop a class or leave the institution altogether. The reasons students leave are many. Food and/or housing insecurities, financial challenges, family obligations, scheduling conflicts, work, and many more.

In *Toward a History of Student Affairs: A Synthesis of Research*, Hevel (2016) confirms that similar concerns impacted student attrition:

> "Student personnel workers" as professional staff in Student Affairs were called reviewed many aspects of the a students' life to help them determine how best to help students and they discovered that "low GPAs, financial struggles, and difficulty adjusting to campus social life led students to leave college, foreshadowing reasons that would be articulated decades later."

What more can be done to increase retention?

For students experiencing academic challenges, the answer is not to relax standards. After all, students are in college to be challenged and to learn. In the meantime, in addition to student data analyses, institutions can also focus on the curriculum to identify ways to make content and delivery more adaptable and accessible. And as a collective think: What might we do differently to help students learn?

Invoking the broken windows theory, a former Forbes contributor, James Marshall Crotty, wrote, referring to the Learning Curve report in 2013 about educational outcomes that "culture, not income, is the ultimate arbiter of academic success." While he suggested this approach for education reform at the elementary and secondary education level, it is not farfetched to entertain in higher education. "We need a CompStat[1] for education, where we can minutely track how a student is performing in the classroom, and whether he or she is at risk of dropping out. We need to be nimble."

Culture when defined broadly can include informal and formal networks that surround a student. If education is more attentive and attuned to students' needs, challenges, skills, and potential, support services can prevail. Some things that can be done outside of the classroom to retain students are as follows:

- Innovate inside and outside the classroom.
- Student loss typically happens early. They feel they can never catch up.
- In the classroom, differentiate instructions and assignments, which can tap into student skills, without sacrificing rigor.

- Use video conferencing as a communication option.
- Follow standardized best practices, so students have a similar or common experience.
- Look at scheduling—how are courses packaged. So there is a balance between writing intensive courses and other time-intensive subject areas, for example.

Other supports that can be scaled up include the following:

- alternative tutoring options,
- supplemental instruction,
- mentoring,
- early alert systems,
- frameworks and benchmarks the likes of Quality Matters,
- use of rubrics,
- instructional design assistance,
- course design and review process, and
- course prep checklists.

A course syllabus dashboard is another tool that surprisingly gets mixed reactions at some colleges, although this tool enables institutions to tracksyllabi uploads and updates, perform routine audits, and ensure that every course has an updated syllabus on record for students. Harvard University, considered the gold standard among higher education institutions, created its own Syllabus Explorer to enable and facilitate syllabi searches. Other adoptions to consider as well include the use of course templates aimed to standardize student navigation experience, accessibility tools, proctoring options and other technologies that offer flexibilty and enhance interactions.

With many colleges expanding their use of learning management systems, having processes in place that respect academic freedoms and also support the student learning experience which impacts retention and student success is an important touch point. Dr. Darcy Hardy, Associate Vice President, Client Success Director at Blackboard, notes that institutions with no course development process, and for example, when every course gets a course shell in the learning management system, have absolutely no control over quality of the course because there is no process in place. The aim for processes, guidelines, and expectations for course design and development is to afford students a consistent learning experience, which includes the visual representation of how and instruction will be delivered.

Also a retention factor is employing a philosophical approach about friendship, which can be relationally applied to mentoring, coaching, and other interactions, is the point of everything, as it can contribute to students' level of connectedness, progress, and success. "For without friends no one would choose to live, though he had all other goods; even rich men and those in possession of office and of dominating power are thought to need friends most of all."[2]

In *Education of an Idealist*, Samantha Power, former United States Ambassador to the United Nations, tells a personal story of her high school days in Georgia and the experiences of some students who were afforded the opportunity to attend schools in more privileged neighborhoods. Students had access, but other factors were inequitable regarding transportation, tutoring, and other supports. Factors that play into a student's success include having direction, support, and resources. Reasons why students have challenges include having little to no direction, an unguided path, confusion, and lack of resources. For just a moment, imagine if before students selected a major, they completed a career quiz, attended a career fair, connected with industry professionals, were part of a mentoring community, and had to pitch their interest and aptitude? Imagine if students could interview for their academic major. While competencies can be learned, imagine if students could hear from potential employers whether or not they have the aptitude and the capacity to handle the material and the skills necessary. While no one would literally stand in the way of a student's dream, imagine how having more insight into the job market, the academic expectations, and the time investment required of that program of study and career would help students?

Success courses can also have a positive impact; in some colleges, they are free, required, or modular, and part of a more extended timeline available at varying occasions during the student's education journey. Many iterations of these courses exist. The goal is to share critical information what it is like to be in college, course expectations, time management, financial literacy, and so on. Usually these courses run 1 week to 15 weeks. But imagine if, pieces of student success modules were available and embedded throughout the student's college experience. Cognizant of student schedules, personal and professional obligations, the goal of this type of module is to build a sense of community for the student. In this scenario, students could have access to many faculty and staff who would essentially become part of their networks.

ANALYTICS, PERSPECTIVES AND ATTITUDES

Dr. Ross Markle, founder and managing director of DIA (Data Information Action) Higher Education Collaborators, shares notable insight that can help institutions move forward in recognizing the importance of building change together because analytics alone are not the answer. Dr. Markle, who held multiple roles at Educational Testing Services, has developed a new assessment tool that is used in a very similar capacity as ETS' Success Navigator, that was retired in September 2019.

Noncognitive assessments help identify branch points that allow institutions to spearhead conversations in putting forward their best effort of holistic advising. The questions asked on these assessments enable an institution to take a close look at a student and learn the student's perspective. While certainly some student responses may not fully disclose everything about the student, at some point, noncognitive details about the student do surface. Use of similar assessments can give colleges more insight about the students. Dr. Markle notes, "It can be a red flag. It enables you . . . on an aggregate and individual level where the challenges seem to be. You may see some trends that may be statistically significant. It can help institutions determine what they can do more about, what they are not doing."

While assessment tools and predictive analytics provide institutions with robust dashboards of information, there is no magic bullet, nor is there one factor that can be addressed that will fix the student's need or enrollment or retention dilemma. Dr. Markle adds, "It's not to say everybody gets two hours of intrusive advising, you have to be able to distinguish who gets that and who doesn't. Because some students need that and some don't. Some students are on the ball and they are ready to identify their transfer institution. And all you need to do is not get in their way."

Dr. Markle speaks more about data attitudes:

When an organization takes the position that certain things are off the table and they are unwilling or unable to consider alternatives in order to make improvements . . . that deficit thinking thwarts the conversation: Process and progress begin at least when the critical mass of the organization expresses its readiness for change. If you think you are going to keep the organization the same and improve results, it's simply impossible. Now that you are ready to change, the question becomes how do you want to make that change happen.

Using data of formal and informal noncognitive assessments, help advance conversations about organizational change by pointing out factors from the student lens. Often changes are rooted in emotion, but survey data qualify the anecdotal and reveal possible branch points and alerts that may require further discussion. "Perhaps there was an issue that maybe they never articulated before. Going through an exercise like process mapping . . . to show them that they are not even aware of what they maybe thought they were. Things like that, where you can pique their interest . . . that's where data are a useful tool in that conversation. And then figuring out what works best. It's just like we say with students, find them where they are . . . take them where we want them to be," elaborates Dr. Markle. That said, assessments should be seen as a tool and not a prescriptive answer.

Regardless of how well some institutions might say they are doing, clearly enrollment and completion data point to concerns and the mindset that the colleges cannot continue doing what they did yesterday. Enrollment data show many colleges are losing as many students as they enroll every semester. "You're like shoveling water out of the boat as its flooding. At best, for the moment, is that 50 percent of students starting at community colleges will ever get a degree or certificate. It's just not good enough," concludes Dr. Markle.

The real question, then, is how do we have a conversation about improving that. The statistics are compelling and warrant a call to action, and that along with establishing a neutral open dialogue can set the tone. Dr. Markle says, "It really starts with the culture and the attitude; the willingness to change is first and foremost." He shares a story about a client institution:

> One year we did an analysis where we looked at development education courses. And we looked at noncognitive skills and performance on the placement test. If you looked at that across all the sections of the course, there was one course where students who had the same level on the placement test, even if they made it into higher level courses, they did way better than if they were at the bottom level of dev ed. Could not isolate if it was instruction. Students who scored the same thing on the placement test and when you put them in higher level courses they do better than in the development ed course.

On a subsequent visit, the following semester the college had stopped placing the students in that course because it wasn't doing anything to help students, shares Dr. Markle.

Modifications can be logical and involve collaboration, curricular and cocurricular innovation, intervention, but as a collective, there is often some level of hesitation. Institutions that are student-focused have a willingness to think how their work impacts students. As colleges ponder the future of higher education, one approach is to reimagine the enrollment process, which will require the cooperation, consultation, and collaboration of faculty and administration. Dr. Markle shares what he called the litmus test: "If you can't convince your faculty that a co-requisite is a good idea, then they are resistant to change. The evidence is so clear that it is a better way of supporting students, when they come in with academic challenges. Anyone who says otherwise is almost irrationally holding to the status quo for whatever reason."

To the extent that colleges are working toward a positive or strength mindset, Dr. Markle comments that another attitudinal challenge that stands in the way of being student-ready and student readiness, and is one of the most difficult to reverse or eradicate is the sentiment or expectation about what students should know. In other words, the blaming of the student. He explains:

Part of the problem is that everyone involved in this conversation were successful in higher ed . . . some of us may have dropped out and come back, or may have started in community college and spun their wheels, especially in higher level position, [or] never had the challenges we are trying to help our students with. And we benefited from the system . . . and so how do we fundamentally question this that came so naturally to us? Most of us graduated in 4 years, maybe went to work or went back to get a masters or PhD.

For most people this system was never foreign to them. For many of the students we are losing, this is a different culture, and the issue is not because they can't be successful; it's that they don't know how to navigate that culture, [which can include unfamiliar words or practices.] For example, the reference to bursar or registrar is uncommon to most incoming students who have not received any orientation. Imagine the difference between a student who goes on a campus visit and that student who simply shows up on the first day, . . . how lost will they be?

From a cultural perspective, there is an attitudinal perspective that is a bigger challenge Dr. Markle addresses and invites higher education to reflect on and question:

If you pick your checklist of traditionally underserved populations . . . if you are a first generation student it's easy not to talk to anyone . . . but if you want to ask a question reach out for help or need some sort of additional support like counseling, those other things that are a bigger lift . . . you have to be confident enough in yourself, you need to be comfortable enough to talk to those people . . . . when you think of it as a culture to which you were not indoctrinated . . .how would you do that?

NOTES

1. CompStat. (n.d.). CompStat 2.0. New York City Police Department. https://ww w1.nyc.gov/site/nypd/stats/crime-statistics/compstat.page.
2. Nicomachean Ethics. http://classics.mit.edu/Aristotle/nicomachaen.8.viii.html.

Chapter 5

Agency and Change

Testing the waters helps students determine if they have aptitude for what they think they want to do. Imagine having students interview for their major? Similar to interviewing for an internship or a job. Imagine what that would do? It could influence the trajectory of that student's life. Understanding student aspirations as well as their challenges and needs assists institutions in navigating student success. Gus Wachbrit, who summarized the CLASSS project findings, aptly submitted in an article *Student Success from the Perspective of Students Themselves*, "Overall, goals relating to socializing and student collaboration are less important to students than goals relating to future endeavors. . . . Foreign students identify GPA and social skill development as more important aspirations than their non-foreign peers. Parents were more likely to identify a career transition as an important goal, while non-parents were more likely than parents to identify transferring to another college or University as a primary goal."[1]

At the Invest Philadelphia conference in November 2019, Pennsylvania, leadership and college presidents shared insights about imperatives to support current and future student success. Takeaways highlighted the importance of access, education and career pathways, infrastructure, and opportunities to reduce equity gaps. Speakers addressed the communication, exchange, and support necessary to advance student success through higher education and business partnerships. They spoke to the changing dynamics of higher education as well as the need to be flexible in order to adapt to the times:

Other comments shared during the conference:

- Awareness of economic requirements needed to retire
- Changing roles means more education, not just training
- Plugging those gaps (with the 60-year curriculum)

- Advising and coaching life and transition management
- The role of advising today is different than before—learner services
- Consolidated career services . . . much more integrated over a life span
- Retention coaching beginning to spread
- Adopt the use of a learning concierge . . . a learning record counselor . . . so you can make the best choice for you.—future
- Expansion of learner services—to help students help themselves beyond college
- Integrate the roles of life coach, career coach, and academic coach into one person that a student can trust
- Potential for badges and certificates
- Recognize that higher ed is not retail, but understand how customer service is just as important
- Lean on colleagues in continuing education for vision and expertise

RISK TAKERS AND LEADERSHIP

Encourage students to keep the end in mind from the beginning. How? Conversations, masterclass engagements, mentoring opportunities, the intangibles.

Brian Gillispie points out in the History of Academic Advising (2003): "Today the services directed toward student development are an amalgamation of their historical components. Measurement and development are still practiced, but under the microscope of accountability, validity and efficiency. An appreciation of the past is an important key to moving academic advising through the next millennium."

So how can institutions become more agile in the arena to help students maximize their potential? Dr. Donald Generals, president of Community College of Philadelphia, says:

> I think a successful approach is design thinking, being a lot more innovative, trying to move away from the hard core traditions embedded in some community colleges that are 55 years old . . . we've got no business being in the tradition business. We don't look at the nature of the learner. Community college students are they different than your typical 4-year institution that for the most part admit students right out of high school. We need to be more focused on needs of the student as opposed to the traditions and structures of the institution, which is what the tendency is right now.

The Community College Research Center (CCRC) reports that "colleges need to consider the ways in which faculty, staff, and college leaders will interact with one another (meetings, emails, case notes) and topics for discussion (reviews of data, discussions of individual student progress) and how this affects responsibilities and work flow. Stakeholders also need training on how to use new technology and how to optimize its functionality to achieve good collaboration" (p. 12).[2]

CCP's Guided Pathways page describes its commitment to ongoing future student success and publicly challenges itself noting: "Students must be prepared to succeed; they must have the support to succeed; and they must have a purpose for succeeding. Failure to encompass those three important elements into conversations about access reduces the concept to an empty promise." Dr. Generals recognizes that "pathways" is just one word but a powerful one that guides institutions in redesigning efforts.

According to CCRC *A framework for Advising Reform*: "In many colleges, both faculty and professional advisors share advising responsibilities but may work in 'silos,' which limits communication and the potential for collaborative relationships. In these cases, close coordination of the work can make sure that the right support options are available to students at each point in their journey through college. In addition, coordination among student support providers of various types (e.g. advising, financial aid, career counseling) can result in better aligned services."[3]

Dr. Joy Gates-Black, president, Delaware County Community College, Media, PA, shares the importance of taking the opportunity to engage students where they are and understanding some of the challenges they experience as they pursue their education. Being aware of student concerns and challenges as well as staying informed about local, regional, national, and international trends are critical in order to make informed decisions that will impact student success. "When an institution that has been around a long time, has an established faculty and staff, it's important to take a moment to take a look national trends, best practices, how are they using data and engaging students. It's a continuous improvement perspective . . . there is always room for improvement," says Dr. Gates Black.

Positive or growth mindset and attitude are important characteristics institutional leaders should embrace. Dr. Gates Black continues:

> Adopting that posture, that kind of business practice for higher-thinking . . . what is it I can do in my classroom and the services we provide? The agility comes from breaking down silos and being open to more collaboration. Gone are the days where I have my piece and you have yours. We have a piece and my piece connects to yours. Students are very fluid in the services they need. All of this has to work together. We have to approach how we are serving our students by working together.

In *Becoming a Student-Ready College*, the authors state: "Students are particularly vulnerable when faculty and administration don't communicate. Yet what if cooperation . . . became a new orthodoxy" (p. 59).

At most community colleges, longevity (several decades of service) exists among professional staff and faculty. Along with that priceless legacy also comes challenge of the present and the uncertain future. A question higher education leaders face is, how to combine the two and meet the needs of the today's students? Simply, leaders experience more success when they are able to engage stakeholders and individuals who want to support and advance student progress together.

Data should serve as a source of information, motivation, and even inspiration. Although for that to work at all levels, the college community should be open to seeing what details the data have to offer that can guide solutions. The idea that students, incoming or returning, need to adapt to the college rather than the college adapting to current student needs is an intransigent approach stemmed from feeling threatened, or from a position of fear or resistance to change, which wastes time and depletes progress.

While presidents are the face of their respective institutions, broad initiative support makes a difference. "It can't just be the president who is the cheerleader," Dr. Gates Black, who has been serving as DCCC's president since 2017, says, "there has been empowerment of people across the college and now most of the change is not being led by me; it may be discussed with me but I'm not the architect of the change, but I'm always the cheerleader. Change is moving on its own to a degree."

In seeking solutions to assist students, a problem not foreign to colleges is conflict. While conflict resolution can almost be an art form in any arena, Dr. Gates Black says, "some conflict is not a bad thing; it shows you are growing."

While institutions reveal varied experiences and challenges, at the core the end goal is the same. Simon Nynens, vice president and chief commercial officer at New Jersey Institute of Technology, and CEO of New Jersey Innovation Institute, an NJIT corporation, speaks regularly to students, business leaders, entrepreneurs, and educators about leadership and key factors that impress success. "While enrollment in community colleges has seen decreases since 2010, 4-year public colleges, and to a lesser extent 4-year independent colleges, have not seen decreases."[4] The student population is declining rapidly, exacerbated by the decline in visas for international students. Whether political or financial, student enrollment is declining nationally although some private and four-year universities are still doing well. NJIT student enrollment, including international student enrollment, continues to show increases. Nynens shares that NJIT's student demographic particularly is more focused. He adds that trend can be attributed to the university's STEM focus and students' competitive desire to be there.

Nynens notes how students from Asia and Egypt, which have a significant population under 24 for example, are facing enormous pressure to educate students. With international unemployment challenges abroad, countries are open markets to recruit students.

The Asia-Pacific region contains 60 percent of the world's youth population, or 750 million young persons aged 15 to 24 years (United Nations).[5] Nynens adds, "We cater to that population. They can't wait to get a job. It's a special student population . . . they don't have the luxury to not know what to do. They are the first or next generation to make it happen. They are focused and driven."

As for the potential domestic applicant pool, Nynens says some students are taking other routes to employment and bypassing or interrupting school; the solution for colleges lies in focusing on what students really want and find a niche. Nynens recommends, as some are already doing, that colleges expand conversations, partnerships, and collaborations with the business community, and in order to better serve students, they should ask employers, "What do you need?" While education pays in the long run, it is an investment some students risk not taking. Some students don't want to go to college any more. Nynens says, "Students need and want a modular approach and some colleges are not prepared for that." And there is a huge demand for retraining, supported by the college noncredit side that offer certificates for areas like cyber security that practically guarantee a job upon completion. Colleges need to continue to create a bridge and other access points between school and business.

Despite criticism and hurdles to overcome by for-profit institutions and online institutions, everyone stands to learn from their successes. "Look at Capella, Southern New Hampshire; they've done really well. Also, some the best programs are hybrid; two weekends and then the rest online. Those face-to-face meetings help faculty build a bond with students," says Nynens.

Advice: Consider the resistors but continue on the quest for alternatives, new ideas and support. Nynens, who sees education as a special industry on the verge of private and public, speaks to the necessity to be open and creative. "Often when you are too insular you won't end up with something new and successful. Tesla ended up with a completely new car which would not have happened had it not been a completely new approach."

As a mentor speaking to both students and organizations, Nynens says, "You have to be much more niche focused. Generalists are dead. In other words, you can have a specialized skill or trade, but also important is the ability to talk to people. That's the challenge." In advising students, Nynens imparts that "it's important to know what you are doing, but it's even more important to know what and why you're doing it. We have to work with the Why. You need to find your Why."

A proponent of the why for all students, MCCC's Dr. Wang is also a believer in colleges having that same type of clarity so they can guide students toward a broader understanding about education:

> The question is how do we provide our students – future employees – with the best skills set closest to employers' expectations. I do not think that workforce readiness has a definitive causal relationship with the academic degree and employability. It really boils down to how we educate. What do we teach them with a technological revolution that is still unfolding. I believe our students need to have the intellectual ability to learn so they can learn while they are here and after they leave us. In their life time, they will have to change jobs multiple times, and if they don't have the ability to learn, when they leave us they will become obsolete.

Looking to the future, education can continue to be relevant by focusing on both cognitive and noncognitive skills. Dr. Wang explains how certain skills in demand for jobs today will shift 5 years from now. In college, a student can learn how to learn, so when they graduate or move on, they can have a sustainable life beyond college. "You can't be in college forever. I think the #1 thing students can do for themselves is to attend. We teach them team work, communication, critical thinking, dealing with difficult people, how to be a change agent . . . and there is not one single course that teaches that. College is the place where you can learn these soft skills," she adds.

In the spirit of continuous learning and the realization that learning ought not to be a finite experience, Dr. Wang shares a Chinese proverb she often says during presentations "half bottles makes a loud noise; full bottle makes no noise" also read as a "half bottle makes noise, while a full bottle makes none" suggests that an empty bottle lacks perspective yet is quick to offer opinions perhaps based on limited knowledge and awareness.

ABOUT CHANGE

Dr. Darcy Hardy, associate vice president, client success director at Blackboard, says, "If the institution as a whole is on board with the mission and the vision of the institution then it seems to me much easier. . . . you bring everyone onboard, then you can start thinking through processes for making changes."

Change management should be transparent, deliberate, and systematic. Dr. Hardy expands:

> Part of having a vision and being a good leader means you're involving the rest of your campus, you're involving your faculty senate, student government, the

registrar . . . you're not mandating, you're leading. The vision for what people want to do only bubbles up from grassroots. However, it's a much harder sell to get that executive leadership to buy into something that is going to force additional resources or rethinking of policy, or how financial resources are going to be spent. While it's great for faculty and staff to have ideas, if they don't have budget authority or the authority to make changes it's probably not going to happen.

Sometimes change meets resistance due to the uncertainty of new expectations and how it may affect various constituencies. "The hardest part of being an effective leader is getting buy-in. Before you announce what you want to do, spend time nurturing that vision by talking to the right people," advises Dr. Hardy:

> Let's say, we have got to make changes to advising. A good leader is going to spend 6–9 months or even a year fostering their ideas with key players, so when it's time to announce the vision he or she already has the right people on board. What doesn't work—you can have a great vision and be extremely innovative, but if you don't nurture the idea with the right people leading up to announcing it and you know you're going to have resistance and you announce it anyway, then you get what you got . . . and get the resistance. A good leader is not going to throw something out and mandate it without having built the buy-in first.

Changes to the status quo is not easy and will meet with resistance; however, communication, being persuasive with your messaging, and not rushing it are strategies to embrace.

Maastricht University (UM), in the Netherlands, has a student population of 18,000 and 4,400 employees. Oscar van den Wijngaard of Maastricht University serves as a project manager on first-year retention. He shares his experiences on effecting advising changes:

> Based on a review of a large part of the student journey through the first year, I have developed recommendations for individual part of this journey, but I am also actively promoting the idea of approaching the issue from the overarching concept of student engagement. My sphere of influence is broad (many stakeholders at different levels), but impact depends on bottom-up support, as each department at my institution has a fair degree of independence and is very protective of it. Central policy is looked at with suspicion, so the fact that my recommendations were approved by the Board of Executive of the university is helpful, but not enough to make change happen. Conceptually, this work is based on the (evidence-based) assumption that student engagement increases student success, both in terms of resilience and academic attainment.

Investing the time on the backend saves time in the long run. To make changes, you need resources and people. Given resource limitations, you need people to buy in; you need people to believe in the idea to make it happen. You really don't do it alone. Cultivate the support and buy-in so the vision becomes theirs as well. Dr. Hardy adds:

> A good strategy to communicate: sit down with groups to talk about what the vision is instead of plowing through . . . being innovative comes with the responsibility of communication and listening, not just having the idea and running with it, but being able to refine and modify it as needed. Consider this scenario: When I'm at a school with a client and we're talking about online, sometimes you see a leader who wants to push multiple programs online in a year, doesn't care which programs, just wants it up and running, and they mandate it and never sit down and talk to anybody about it. So then you have the campus scrambling trying to figure out what that leader really wants . . . that's a huge problem and often turns people off on the whole idea of doing alternate program because it was mandated, without thinking about process, oversight, without involving key players and stakeholder, just making a decision and washing their hands of it and expecting everybody to somehow make it all happen.

So how you move the need around innovation leads back to having a vision, a good communication plan, and what it means to have good quality. Engage faculty in conversations, and encourage collegial exchanges to share what other institutions are doing successfully toward supporting student success.

NOTES

1. Gus Wachbrit (October 23, 2019). Student Success from the Perspective of Students Themselves. Social Science Space. Retrieved from https://www.socialsciencespace.com/2019/10/student-success-from-the-perspective-of-students-themselves/.

2. CCRC A framework for Advising Reform (2019, July). Retrieved from https://files.eric.ed.gov/fulltext/ED597852.pdf.

3. CCRC A framework for Advising Reform (2019, July). Retrieved from https://files.eric.ed.gov/fulltext/ED597852.pdf.

4. American Association of Community Colleges. Community College Enrollment Crisis: Historical Trends in Community College Enrollment. Retrieved from https://www.aacc.nche.edu/wp-content/uploads/2019/08/Crisis-in-Enrollment-2019.pdf.

5. Economic and Social Commission for Asia and the Pacific (UNESCAP). Regional Overview: Youth in Asia and the Pacific. https://www.un.org/esa/socdev/documents/youth/fact-sheets/youth-regional-escap.pdf.

Chapter 6

Mission Accomplishing

Sustaining the future of academe involves the preservation of *lernfreiheit*, the freedom to learn for students and respect toward *lehrfreiheit*, freedom of teaching or academic freedom supported by leadership who have the best interest of both at the forefront of institutional priorities. A capable and nimble organizational structure can uphold this delicate balance.

In *American Higher Education: A History*, Christopher J. Lucas (1996) details the roots of academe and catalogs debates, issues, and challenges this industry has faced, some of which still resonate today. Mobilizing efforts, for example, to provide nonacademic resources and support to students' current needs is an area that institutions are investing time and finances realizing that inaction can have negative implications and may preclude students from pursuing and continuing their education. Lucas writes:

> Contemporary institutions of higher depend on three main sources for funding, private, gifts, research grants and contracts, tuition payment . . . in other words they depend upon outside benefactors, upon business or government and upon the market. Dependence, as has often been argued, spells vulnerability to influence. . . . Hence the question has become in what ways institutions of higher learning can protect themselves from corrupting influences . . . while preserving for themselves the autonomy needed for the pursuit of learning. By the same token, the question is also one of balance between institutional independence and responsiveness to social need. (p. 307)

All things being equal in a discussion or debate, reason tends to prevail even if there are latecomers to the table. However inflexible the resistance that plays out in higher education, reason aside, because it can, has debilitating effects on student and institutional success, which are holistically one and the same. So what might be the way to rally to make a change? Simon Nynens submits that there is no magic formula either: "It's an art . . . people are people. We fear change, and need to build alliances." The question about managing higher education institutions like a business is debatable, but the consideration that many leaders are closely reflecting, realizing that modeling some business practices might be useful. Nynens iterates, "It's a special industry on the verge of private and public."

ITERATIVE IMPROVEMENTS AND STRATEGIES

In *Show Me the Way: The Power of Advising in Community Colleges 2018 Report*, testimonials featured accounts of institutions that have successfully made significant modifications to previous ways of handling retention and completion demands. Making provisions to build a community of support for students that are grounded in appreciative inquiry has led many of these institutions to begin to see positive outcomes. Beyond academic planning, for example, considering noncognitive factors as an additional measure of student success has enhanced the scope of advising. Equally important is the conversation of career paths at all points during a student's journey, not just at the point of graduation.

The 2018 Strada-Gallup Alumni Survey: Mentoring College Students to Success sought to learn about the graduates' experiences during college and postgraduation. The survey examined the perceptions of 5,100 U.S. college graduates, and it validates the importance of student well-being, personal relationships, sense of community, connectedness, academic rigor, and career guidance while in college. A strength-based approach can help institutions develop integrated services that support and "leverage" student skills and talents that empower them to reach "previously unattained levels of personal excellence."[1]

Once institutions self-assess and have gathered data that allow them to look inward, what's next? It must be a continuous process. In the spirit of holistic advising, institutions have to advise themselves and analyze themselves holistically before attempting to advise a student holistically. In a 2013 TEDxFSU, Dr. Kathleen Shea Smith (presently associate provost for Academic Advising at the University of Oklahoma), who was at the time associate director of Advising First, the network of academic advisors and success coaches at Florida State University, delivered a thoughtful speech about working and supporting the inner student. She celebrated and highlighted the critical nature of the advising experience and, more importantly, how institutions should "create staying conditions so that students are not just surviving but thriving." While her presentation was seven years ago, the message resonates with the ongoing work needed and taking place in education. With the recent COVID-19 pandemic, institutions are toggling among some many equally important priorities: continuing to serve students, continuing to stay in business despite the disruptive interruption of social distancing, and thoughts about the future and how the current model of education might never be the same again.

In Dr. Smith's presentation, she speaks to Vicente Tinto's institutional departure model[2] and notes how institutions must take responsibility and think about how to self-motivate each other to fix the system. In addition, she shares the importance of informal networks, how meaningful connections are what matters most, and, lastly, the benefit of having "leadership that cares about advising and invests in advising [to] build relationships that are continuous."[3] During less eventful times, the focus relationships may not get as much attention, but institutions with foresight have a better chance of success than others whose shift are reactionary.

According to a College Board report Education Pays 2019, "Among undergraduate students who started college for the first time in 2011-12, 66% of those whose first enrollment was at a public 4-year institution and 77% of those who started at a private nonprofit 4-year institution completed either an associate or a bachelor's degree within 6 years. In contrast, 32% of public 2-year students and 23% of for-profit students completed an associate or bachelor's degree within 6 years."[4] While there are many factors that have contributed to these numbers, one in particular that is consistently mentioned is course scheduling—in other words, offering courses at times convenient to students. With student work-life responsibilities, it is important for colleges to determine student availabilty for course scheduling. Surveying students to identify a range of availability can make a difference for students and for enrollment.

In *Understanding the Student Experience through the Loss/Momentum Framework: Clearing the Path to Completion*, published by the Research & Planning Group for California Community Colleges, authors Elisa Rassen, Priyadarshini Chaplot, and Rob Johnstone, founder and president of the National Center for Inquiry and Improvement (NCII), and Davis Jenkins, of Community College Research Center, discussed how course scheduling could make a difference in student success. They advised how institutions could do a better job of coordinating the scheduling process so that students have suitable options.

> The schedule for the upcoming semester is likely put together far in advance based on numerous different factors, each of which is located in a different part of the institution. These factors often include administrative management of course fill rates and associated costs; faculty availability; student demand;

classroom or lab availability; . . . However, the student engages with all of those components in a singular experience: she or he needs to be able to enroll in a specific course to meet the requirements of a program of study. When that course is unavailable because the numerous "ingredients" of the course schedule have all come from separate silos, the student's future can be derailed.[5]

Efforts such as course scheduling, on-campus programming, advising approaches and events, and campus-wide initiatives such as updating a college's strategic plan should be coordinated and communicated to prevent silos. Dr. Nutt, of NACADA, expands on this approach as it regards to advising, saying: "this is not a one and done activity." Redesigning or updating advising to be more well-rounded and holistic is continuous work, an iterative process. He says that institutions have to consider what they want to achieve and develop a comprehensive focus.

"We oftentimes do an activity that sits on a shelf and in five years no one knows we've done that. So it's really making this a comprehensive approach a continuing approach, not we've done this once and we don't have to do it again," adds Dr. Nutt. An example of this could be institutional technology investments that are not comprehensively adopted or implemented, which can be reflective of minimal or a lack of buy-in.

In *Evolving Higher Education Business Models: Leading with Data to Deliver Results*, former Stanford University vice president for business and finance Stanford University, William F. Massy, underscores in the foreword: "The new leaders 'awaken' networks of faculty, administrators, and others—both within institutions and across groups of institutions—to create deeper insights about best practices and financial consequences. These networks exist already, but they operate in an uncoordinated fashion without benefit of common data. Indeed, the paucity and concentration of data mean that even shared governance (a kind of network) works mainly through proxies rather than wide participation."[6]

Another mindset that needs to shift is that about teaching and how everyone on campus has the capacity to be an effective educator, as elaborated in the book *Becoming a Student-Ready College* (2016). This suggests that learning takes place in and outside the classroom. That means that advising, which impacts student progress, can also be considered teaching.

Usually confined to an aspect of student affairs or student services, Dr. Nutt agrees and raises the point that advising is teaching and learning, and not a service. He believes it should be everyone on campus that has that opinion. "It should matter not who is delivering the advising; it should matter how advising supports student learning." Given the perspective that echoed from the beginning, essentially, everyone can potentially have a role in holistic advising and so there is no need for anyone to feel territorial that someone is encroaching on an area. He says, "Absolutely, but you can't do that unless you have a campus-wide approach to looking at these things."

In order to arrive at consensus about advising, institutions should consider the types of inquiries, transactions, or needs students might have in a semester. According to Matson and Robinson, "Students should have six strengths-based touchpoints a year with a friend, mentor, adviser or professor—anyone who deliberately helps students direct their strengths—to live a more engaged and thriving life. These touchpoints don't have to be new. You can integrate them into the programs and organizations that already exist on your campus."[7] The point is that there is no prescribed way for an institution to accomplish this. Institutions should have the freedom to be creative and support this in a way their organizational culture can uncompromisingly follow through.

There isn't a silver bullet answer that will identify the exact journey or steps. By having conversations and learning what colleagues are doing and the challenges they face, campus communities can become a little bit more flexible and fluid in finding alternatives and solutions. This approach can cultivate a working rapport that is productive and disposed to meet the students' diverse needs. Moreover, the humility to consider as much information as possible to expand the breadth and depth of knowledge about students is critical. A recent Lipman Hearne study identified the personas of adult learners (reinventors, scholars, change makers, and seekers)[8] with the goal of helping institutions better understand, recruit, and serve the needs of this population, which comprises more than a quarter of undergraduate enrollment.[9]

To compartmentalize students and roll over strategies that worked seamlessly in the past is unproductive and will not yield the results institutions need to advance. Every student is different and has a different story to tell. Dr. Ted Mitchell, president of the American Council on Education, describes today's student as not fitting into a particular model. "The new normal student is just as likely to be a twenty-five-year-old returning veteran, a thirty-year-old single parent, or a fifty-three-year-old displaced worker who is looking to reskill and retrain."[10] And he adds that it would serve higher education well, if it were to listen to what guidance students afford: "they expect and accept that technology will be an important and helpful part of their college/university experience."

Building the capacity by leveraging technology and creating a sustainable ecosystem to consistently provide meaningful connections between students and the institution is attainable and necessary. As institutions work to enhance the student experience by weaving awareness of the broader scope of their needs and future expectations of the job market, similarly colleges must work harmoniously and optimize efforts to maximize progress in preparing students for life beyond college.

The Community College Research Center's (CCRC) evidence-based framework for advising redesign, SSIPP, stands for sustained, strategic, integrated, proactive, and personalized advising. "The SSIPP framework is largely derived from a review of the literature on institutional services and interventions, including academic advising, that aim to help students navigate college and take into account academic and nonacademic aspects of the student experience."

A scan of advising systems across colleges reveals myriad compositions and organizational reporting structures. In some cases, advising is in part a function of admissions and enrollment services, counseling, or found under the purview of either student services or academic affairs. Wherever it resides, awareness of the role advising plays throughout the student life cycle should be considered so all involved work is in coordination. *Show Me the Way: The Power of Advising Community Colleges* noted that "as less than 50% of first-time-in-college students return to the same institution the following fall, this discrepancy suggests that early advising might contribute to increased retention. Also half of the students who consider transferring have never used college transfer advising services."[11] Consequently, meeting with the same advisor throughout is helpful to cultivating a student's sense of belonging, which can positively impact retention. Given scheduling challenges, a way to address this can be group advising or communities where a number of different faculty and staff can be involved as connections for the student.

Based on suggestions published in *Show Me the Way: The Power of Advising in Community Colleges 2018* national report, questions higher education institutions should consider when thinking about ways to improve student advising experiences are as follows:

- How can all students be advised each term and prior to each term?
- How has the advising role changed at your institution?
- What new expectations are there for advisors?
- How can successful smaller-scale intrusive advising models be scaled up?

Community College of Philadelphia, for example, upgraded its advising to include full-time advisors who are assigned to students in addition to faculty who advise on a part-time basis. They use in-person and virtual advising via Skype, Starfish, and first-year experience courses and have seen increased persistence rates among first time in college students. Also, the use of technology can leverage interactions so that more students are able to get more in-depth advising, such as in the case of Mercer County Community College and Delaware County Community College.

In addition to advising interactions, high-impact practices are known to positively affect students. A list of high-impact practices include first-year seminars diversity/global learning, experiential learning experiences, learning communities, writing-intensive courses, service learning and community-based learning, e-portfolios to undergraduate research (Kuh, 2008). Services that demonstrated varying degrees of success toward student persistence include frequent advisor meetings, supplemental instruction, tutoring, scholarships, and developmental education programs. *What Really Works: A Review of Student Success Initiatives* reported: "The abundance of intelligence theoretically available to every level of an institution should suggest more meaningful improvements in the persistence, retention, and graduation rates of all student groups. Because of budget challenges, a pressure to avoid risk, and some analytical limitations, this work will not happen overnight."[12]

Ultimately, the goal of redesign is to have a formation that is interconnected and operates cohesively where the role of advising and/or coach has stretched to buttress the students' current support needs. ACE's Mitchell writes in the article "Transform: Changing Demographics and Digital Transformation": "To meet the needs of our students at this time of change and challenge, we cannot simply do things the old way. . . . We need to embrace a level of change that is transformative and that capitalizes on the digital tools at hand and coming down the line."

Aim to engage the college community at all levels to align buy-in, efforts, and support. Similarly, streamlined data collection with an understanding about how to unpack and share that information can help institutions advance a plan or strategic intervention that is targeted and holistic.

UNPACKING DATA

As many colleges can attest to, worse than siloed communication is siloed data, which keeps members of the college community in the dark. The goal is to avoid disparate data and communication, and interactions. To that end, there are companies that specialize in data science and work with higher education institutions to help them navigate, synthesize, and analyze data that can help guide decision-making.

Civitas Learning, a data science company, focuses on improving high education outcomes via its Student Success Intelligence Platform (SSIP). This platform collects and analyses student data for the purpose of providing insight to student support systems. In its *What Really Works: A Review of Student Success Initiatives* report, Civitas reviewed the impact of a scan of 1,000 student success initiatives in 55 institutions and found that while efforts abound, a more coordinate approach would have been more helpful. "The fact that many services that were not impactful for the student body at large but were effective for a small subset of students is not surprising, especially considering today's educational environment, where roughly 75 percent of students fit into one or more 'non-traditional' category. Services that were designed for the student body of the past may not have the same impact on the students of today." While this does not mean that efforts in place have no merit, it does suggest that plans should be inclusive of stakeholder feedback, and qualitatively and quantitatively mindful. Dr. Sue Ohrablo recommends in *High Impact Advising*, "By developing reports that provide advisors critical information about their advisees, institutions can offer advisors the tools they need to effectively assist students . . . use these tools to comprehensively and proactively assist students and remove unnecessary barriers they may encounter" (p. 199).

The reports, however, should be accessible and updated routinely in order for the data to be useful to retention efforts. There should also be a plan in place that considers the types of information that are critical to end users and the intention behind access to this information. In other words, armed with knowledge, what is the next step. For instance, if there is data that identifies students who possess close to the number of credits required to graduate, or there is a list showing students who are missing key financial aid verification components, what is the plan? What is the plan for outreach, how will these students be notified, and who will own the responsibility for following through?

International students come to mind, as it represents a significant population for higher education enrollments. During transitional times where they may not be able to travel abroad to further their education, how can institutions continue to serve them? For many international students, placement into college-level English can be a challenge. Consequently, they can spend too much time enrolled in English as a Second Language courses before they actually get to matriculate in what they enrolled in college to begin with. So what can colleges do? Perhaps, leverage noncredit courses to create a preparatory bridge so that international students can more successfully test into college-level courses. Integrating publisher materials that feature adaptive learning, or emporium models coupled with embedded online tutoring, could help move the needle of success for students.

Data enables institutions to widen their aperture. It can be helpful to institutions to increase insight about their students. Ellucian CRM Advise, in its white paper *Evolving Early Alerts Early Engagement*, also supports this perspective about the importance of using student data as a means to identify new priorities and successes, noting that "this type of data use can empower colleges to reach out by name those students who are at-risk or in need, as well as those who should be complemented and rewarded."

It listed the positive experiences of Muskegon Community College, Howard University, and Delta State University, which increased targeted outreach and retention based on the insight the data afforded them. "For nearly 20 years, campuses have identified individual 'at-risk' students—often based on poor grades, attendance, or participation. It's a valuable practice worth continuing, but it has its limitations."[13] In addition, the white paper suggested:

- "increased access to evidence-based practices, data and analytics, and technology allows institutions to proactively connect with a larger population of students in a meaningful way before they exhibit signs of trouble. Thus, institutions can more effectively monitor and promote students' participation in educationally effective or high impact practices that encourage engagement and success."
- "expanding to an early engagement process allows institutions to be intentional, help students earlier, and communicate more effectively." (Ellucian)

NONCOGNITIVE DATA POINTS

DIA's ISSAQ (Incoming Student Skills and Attitudes Questionnaire) System, designed to support student retention, persistence, and success in higher education, collects nonacademic data that adds to having a greater understanding about where students are and where they have been. The assessment gathers data on the following noncognitive factors: behavioral, motivational, emotional, and social. ISSAQ assessment addresses an array of noncognitive skills such as engagement, persistence, stress and coping, and sense of belonging.

DIA submits questions that higher educations should ask themselves in order to frame actionable plans that work best to support students.

- How do we understand the meaningful strengths and challenges our students bring to college?
- How do we relate that understanding to student success outcomes?
- How do we support students to actually improve their likelihood for success?

DIA's Dr. Markle points out that in other words: "we are very good at identifying who succeeds and who doesn't, but less able to identify why some students succeed and others don't. And that is where there should be more concentrated efforts." He adds that noncognitive skills or constructs are important for many reasons.

In *Non-Cognitive Skills and Factors in Educational Success and Academic Achievement*, Myint Khine (2016) noted that this type of data:

provides researchers with a manageable set of constructs to investigate; it helps educators and other practitioners focus on a key set of developable constructs; it gives policymakers a clear set of constructs to integrate into future education programs and policy decisions; and it presents employers with a larger pool of potential employees that exhibit the types of skills they want. (p. 14)

Conversations with potential employers and a scan of job descriptions highlight both industry-specific skills plus a range of noncognitive characteristics that demonstrate fluency in critical thinking, team work, innovation, emotional intelligence, analysis, organization, and problem-solving. Kline notes that "there is a perceived mismatch between what students are learning at school and what people need to succeed in the workforce . . . which grows more evident over time as the demands of employers shift to accommodate changes in technology and the markets" (pp. 14–15). Consequently, employers are looking more to higher education partnerships to fill gaps in their applicant pool.

In *Fostering and Measuring Skills: Improving Cognitive and Noncognitive Skills to Promote Life Time Success*, Kautz, Heckman, Diris, Weel, and Borghans (2014) submitted that noncognitive skills, as skills can be learned, develop and change over time, which should serve as a reminder to education of how valuable a role it can and should take on in assessing those skills as well. Kautz, Heckman, Diris, Weel, and Borghans (2014) note that "effective policies to promote skills straddle the missions of cabinet agencies and draw on the wisdom of many academic disciplines. They require broad thinking and recognition that both cognitive and non-cognitive skills are important ingredients of successful lives and are malleable to different degrees at different stages of the life cycle" (p. 10.) First-year experiences, coaching, mentoring, leadership opportunities, and ongoing student-college exchanges can build on these critical skills.

In *Seven Facts on Noncognitive Skills from Education to the Labor Market* (2016) Diane Whitmore Schanzenbach, Ryan Nunn, Lauren Bauer, Megan Mumford, and Audrey Breitwieser also bring light to how equally important, but not as recognized as cognitive skills, are the noncognitives, to a student's life-time success. "The value of these qualities in the labor market has increased over time as the mix of jobs has shifted toward positions requiring noncognitive skills. Evidence suggests that the labor-market payoffs to noncognitive skills have been increasing over time and the payoffs are particularly strong for individuals who possess both cognitive and noncognitive skills" (Deming 2015; Weinberger 2014). The need for collaboration, team building, and interpersonal communication in various modalities is indicative of this growing requirement in the labor market.

Fast technological advances are changing the jobs of the future, which continuously challenges educators to stay current and aim to prepare students as much as possible with critical skills aligned with the needs of the job market. Schanzenbach, Nunn, Bauer, Mumford, and Breitwieser (2016) note that "the educational system may not be focused on the skills that are in demand now and are likely to be in demand in the future. Teachers and schools are held accountable for the cognitive skill levels and growth of their students as measured by standardized tests" (p. 1). While specific industry skills are particularly necessary in certain fields and can be supported at intervals by training or retraining, in the meantime, colleges can always cultivate noncognitive skill awareness throughout a student's college stay.

While workforce demand–curricula alignment is easier said than done, ongoing communication with businesses helps to build the bridge between education and the workforce by way of partnerships, experiential learning, guest lecturers, career events, internships, apprenticeships, and more. A recent survey of hiring managers suggests that they are at least as concerned by deficits in noncognitive skills as they are by lack of cognitive skills (PayScale 2016). While job market needs and trends outpace curriculum development, communities of practice and exchanges with business leaders can serve students well. An article in *the Harvard Business Review* reported, "Given that students today will experience an average of 11.9 career changes over their lifetimes, half of which will occur between the ages of 18–24, colleges and universities must partner with business and industry to develop the skills that will prepare our students not only for a wide range of workplace options, but that will also equip them to deal with a future none of us can fully predict" (Pasquerella, 2019).

In *Defense of a Liberal Education*, Fareed Zakaria submits that he asked Jeff Bewkes, CEO of Time Warner, what skill was considered most useful in business. His reply was, "Teamwork. You have to know how to work with people and get others to want to work with you. It's probably the crucial skill, and yet education is mostly about solo performance" (p. 69).

A SYSTEMS APPROACH

Organizational change is fueled by the openness to embrace needs, deficiencies, and demand, in order to develop a transparent, coherent, interoperational, cross-functional support system that aims to avoid or minimize pitfalls of the past. For example, coordinated student reminders to move from singular, last-minute visits with students (typically close to registration) to ongoing touch points can make a difference. While ideally, increased interactions, high-impact practices suggest a need for more personnel, often that is not possible given budgetary limitations. However, it is achievable by way of system-wide technical supports and a student cohort-based model that can help with organizing "sustained engagement" and case management. Technical options include: one-way and two-way texting, nudge hubs for key student reminders, video conferencing for individual or group e-advising, use of the learning management system, early alert systems, predictive analytics platforms, advising software, and appointment scheduling software.

According to CCRC (2017, February) *What We Know about Technology-Mediated Advising Reform*, advising-related technology can help advisors who have large number of advisees, in some cases as many as 1,200. CCRC notes, "The most compelling evidence in favor of e-advising . . . comes from a study of 13,555 across 8 non profit colleges that used InsideTrack. InsideTrack, since 2001[,] contributed coaching models to improving persistence and completion of traditional, community college military, online and underrepresented students." Forms of communication include "phone calls and personalized texts to help students set goals, identify connections between short and long term goals, learn self advocacy and improve time management and study skills." Results showed that students who were coached persisted more than uncoached students.

CCRC reported that the Minnesota Office of Higher Education, for example, experienced more than 30 percent retention and graduation of students from technical and vocational programs coached after first year of mentoring with Inside Track. But technology alone is not the answer. "Changes to one dimension without changes to the other will not fundamentally alter how a college operates" (p. 2).

INNOVATION IMPERATIVES

At the writing of this book, the coronavirus was spreading nationwide and internationally. The growing number of people testing positive, 17.7 million cases in the United States, the 300,000 plus deaths[14] associated, and the threat of exposure and spread have affected politics, the stock market, and education, with school districts closing, colleges cancelling classes, or instruction unexpectedly moving entirely online as a precautionary and indefinite measure. George Siemens writes in his book *Knowing Knowledge*, "Change forces change."

While some institutions may have already possessed emergency preparedness protocol for unforeseen circumstances like this, pre-planning may have been a head-start. For others, with no contingency plan, last-minute coordination could backfire given limited opportunity for reflection or deliberation. The jury is still out on what impact institutional decisions made will have on enrollment and retention, but the point is that a visceral circumstance such as COVID-19 has been the driver behind previously difficult conversations. The result has been creative and coordinated planning and some level of risk taking that has happened in order to continue to serve students without much disruption.

A proponent of connectivism, knowledge sharing, and assessment that contribute a change implementation cycle, Siemens notes that to "tinker around the edges, in constant conflict with the balance of the organization, is a taxing and frustrating process" (p. 128). In the case of the coronavirus pandemic situation, colleges that did not consider course delivery online in the past, and institutions where use of remote learning technologies experienced varying levels of resistance, concurred that education technology could turn out to be a strategic solution to keep things moving. This pandemic has forced institutions to actionably and purposefully deliberate, rally, learn, adopt, adapt, and change, if not just temporarily, in order to continue to serve students as their survival depends on it.

Siemens writes: "Our organizational spaces and structures have been designed to serve an era that no longer exists . . .We have to unlearn what no longer serves us well . . . we must walk forward with an adaptive mindset — recognizing pattern changes and adjusting as the environment itself adjusts" (p. 143). Unfortunately, it takes life-altering events to see visible movements reflecting real conversations that lead to behavioral and system changes.

In *Wired for Success: Real World Solutions for Transforming Higher Education* (2014), authors Susan C. Aldridge and Kathleen Harvatt challenge the status quo in a truth-telling narrative about the pressures facing higher education, the innovation imperative, the courageous leadership needed and those who have been answering the call to action. A frequent keynote speaker, and accomplished higher education leader, strategist, and futurist, Dr. Susan Aldridge, writes:

> Many presidents and chancellors inherit administrators, faculty and staff who have not only outlasted several presidencies, but have also spend decades steeped in institutional tradition that precludes competitive advantage in a market driving, higher education environment. On top of that, they are frequently confronted with outdated instructional modalities, lackluster programs, and inefficient support services -- not to mention millions of dollars in deferred maintenance, inadequate endowment, and unsustainable business models. . . . Although boards of trustees are generally willing to support campus change (in spite of faculty reluctance or in some cases, downright opposition), their aspirations often outpace institutional capacity.

In a 2020 blogpost, Dan Greenstein, Pennsylvania's State System of Higher Education (PASSHE) chancellor, noted the good work underway to address the current challenges presented by the pandemic. "I am every day impressed by the quality, talent, commitment and good intent of our faculty and staff. Still, for whatever reason, we have been slow to evolve in ways that enable us to meet the dramatically changing needs of our students, their employers, our communities and the state" (Chancellor's Blog, February 13, 2020 http://chancellorgreenstein.blogspot.com/).

Generally speaking, the enrollment issue and the additional impalement of the coronavirus is borderless, affecting the educational operational engine of higher education. To that end, the PASSHE chancellor recognizes how higher education could have been better prepared to handle this current crisis if it had not operated from a "strategy of hope" that students would continue to enroll even when the trend has been pointing downward. "This pattern became unsustainable years ago, but until now we have not had the courage to address it. . . . for years—even decades—students showed up every fall and filled our course sections," writes the PASSHE chancellor. Despite the high stakes challenges, Chancellor Greenstein shares nuggets of optimism:

> We will look forward, not backward. Work together, not alone. Act from trust, not from enmity. In time and through our successes we will learn to let go of the hurt and animosity and blame that continue to show up in some places to negatively influence our culture. . . . I see it in thoughtful, constructive, and collegial dialog with leadership of our faculty union, APSCUF, with whom we have a shared understanding of and a profound commitment to the "why" of our change journey. . . . I see it in our university leadership—in their thoughtful and analytically driven university strategies and budgets; their willingness to roll up sleeves and help one another; their openness to adopting collaborative approaches to individual institutional challenges; their energy for change leadership; their collegiality with one another; and their thought partnership with me. (Chancellor's Blog, February 13, 2020 http://chancellorgreenstein.blogspot.com/)

Wired for Success reminds leaders and advocates for needed education changes that only together can innovation be successfully and comprehensively accomplished. While risk-takers, as CCP's president points out, are necessary, they too have to build relationships and garner support to advance cohesively. In addition, there is a need for open-mindedness, transparency and the capacity to evaluate situations and problem solve through multiple lenses. For example, the need to streamline course offerings can be painstaking but necessary at a time where enrollment and financial aid limitations do not support so many options.

Consequently, course schedules should be representative of what students need and not just what faculty want to teach. According to *Wired for Success*, "this boutique approach" to course development provides a fascinating array of learning options but the "behavior is less conducive to 21st century education," which can be enhanced by interdisciplinary collaboration and best-practice sharing. Perspectives from the 2015 American Council on Education (ACE) and the TIAA Institute roundtable opined: "For organizations with a social mission, such as colleges and universities, he [Peter Drucker] posited that systematic approaches to change based on good data, insight, and leadership would allow for innovation with integrity through which institutions might improve the lives of the individuals they serve."[15]

Cheryl Hyman, author of *Reinvention: The Promise and Challenge of Transforming a Community College System* (2018), published: "We need agents of change in leadership positions, not administrators who know there are failures in the system but are loath to or unable to disrupt the status quo ... leaders. Worse than taking risks that don't pan out is not taking risks at all, hesitating out of fear of criticism and retaliation" (p. 142). The ACE-TIAA roundtable paper explained that courage, foresight, and a sensibility toward a business model approach in higher education are characteristics networked leaders need to possess to advance necessary changes:

> It requires presidents and other institutional leaders to have a simple means for understanding their business model and a networked organization way of thinking . . . while empowering frontline staff, faculty, and administrators to make informed decisions that serve the institutional mission. College and university leaders will need to engage in the hard work of extracting actionable information from the data in their information systems, leading their faculty and staff to understand and articulate the real relationships between their inputs and outputs as an organization, and then executing informed decisions driven by mission, quality, cost, and revenue considerations. The construction of such a network will ultimately allow leaders and their institutions to realize the benefits of efficient, cost-saving measures and pursue business model innovations that could meaningfully improve affordability, accessibility, learning outcomes, degree production, and institutional health. (p. 2)

Blackboard's Dr. Darcy Hardy, who also serves on the United States Distance Learning Association's Board of Directors, highlights leadership characteristics that truly move mountains are those that take the time to foster collaboration and buy-in. Typically, mandated implementations don't flourish, however, when certain operational or technological changes are imperative to the sustainability of the college, reason must prevail. If resistance is grounded on a lack of skills by certain stakeholders, then leadership much consider alternative options for the greater good of the institution and students, she notes.

The bottom line is that necessity breeds creativity. As of July 2020 reported in the *Chronicle* are more than 50,000 employees across over 200 institutions that have resorted to layoffs, contract nonrenewals due to the COVID-19 pandemic.[16] Other casualties have been in the form of budget cuts, paring down of academic programs, the elimination of faculty[17] and staff positions,[18] salary reductions, salary and hiring freezes, retirement contribution suspension, mergers, state system institution pairing,[19] and closures. Not all these outcomes can be said to be causal to COVID-19 as these institutions may still have been experiencing challenges that due to the current state made situations less tolerable.

The exigencies of graduation rates, retention, and enrollment trends represent symptoms in need of redress. In that vein, colleges should also be open to partnership and consultations that can provide or complement expertise needed to advance changes. Recognizing institutional and student needs, and the talent necessary to troubleshoot and move forward calls for leadership that has deep roots and support to withstand resistance and shoulder growing pains of change.

In *Wired for Success*, Dr. Aldridge writes:

> As desirable as it may be to open new niche market and adopt novel instructional methods, both require a level of commitment and expertise that commitment and expertise that isn't "always available in-house . . . .. Facing lower enrollment . . . institutions are pouring exorbitant amounts into expensive marketing tools . . . and search engine optimization. As a result, the cost of recruiting students has doubled in the last few years, and retention rates continue to fall short of expectations. Thus without the captive student audiences they have always relied on, postsecondary institutions must also find more effective ways to attract new students.

Attracting new students as well as keeping enrollments as steady as possible, especially during challenging times, tests the adaptability, flexibility, and capacity of institutions and its thought leaders. The goal is to express to students with clarity why higher education is a viable answer. Inarguably, reasons students share for pursuing an education or taking a gap semester or more are work-related. Consequently, leading with discussions about career and aligning academic options with students' personal outcomes is critical.

These conversations as many leading or operating in the advising space comment should take place at the gate, from the first advising session. In other words, the labor market value of education can be impressed upon students through holistic advising. *The Overlooked Value of Certificates and Associate's Degrees: What Students Need to Know Before They Go to College*, a new report from the Georgetown University Center on Education and the Workforce (CEW), an independent, nonprofit research, and policy institute that studies the link between individual goals, education and training curricula, and career pathways, reveals that certificates and certifications "outearn" associates degrees.

The Georgetown University Center study found that the combined number of certificates and associate's degrees awarded by colleges, two million, is similar to the number of bachelor's degrees awarded per year. The study reported that workers across 10 states—Colorado, Connecticut, Indiana, Kentucky, Minnesota, Ohio, Oregon, Texas, Virginia, and Washington—with associate's degrees in engineering technologies and health professions earn more than workers who have an associate's degrees in other fields across most states.

The lesson to be understood here is about education consumer value. This means recognizing that individuals seek opportunity, learning, or otherwise that can lead them to gainful employment—a career. As defined, the "education consumer value equation is the relationship between what an individual perceives to be the cost value and career value of their education."[20]

In *True Value: A New Model for Measuring the Value of Postsecondary Education by Listening to Americans: Survey of 340,000 Adults Informs Creation of Strada Education Consumer Value Equation, Providing New Insight into Learners' Needs and Priorities* (2019), Sarah J. Bauder, chief transformation officer for the Pennsylvania State System of Higher Education, states, "The data is telling policymakers, employers and educators alike that students in any major, from engineering to English to psychology, want to know how to connect their learning to a future job. We must work together to better help learners make those connections through advising, mentoring and applied learning." "As they consider investing their time, money and hopes in postsecondary education, consumers need to see that it will connect them with a purposeful pathway. That's when they find value."[21]

The commitment necessary to advance education pursuits is akin to the future value of money. Students are willing to invest with the belief that it will pay off in the future by way of career, compensation, and additional opportunity. The full report *Changing the Value Equation in Higher Education* (2019) points to the "strong connection between learning and careers when consumers find their courses are relevant to work, when they receive high-quality, applied-learning experiences and excellent career and academic advising."[22]

Advising at all stages of the student's academic journey inarguably impacts student success. The capacity to outreach thousands of students at a time and digital tools that enhance communication and engagement with the aim that no student is left behind are critical and necessary components of systemic advising process. At the top of *EDUCAUSE Top10 IT* issues continues to be

Student Success and Student Centered Institution, yet "the three big questions remain: how to define, measure, and structure student success, all while keeping the student at the center," writes Kathe Pelletier in *Student Success: 3 Big Questions*. "Technology is one part of student success initiatives, but it's not as simple as just plugging in a degree-planning tool. A strategically designed data ecosystem that includes a data warehouse to capture information from a variety of systems inside and outside the classroom—CRM, SIS, LMS, and even SSMS (student success management system)—and across the lifecycle, from recruitment to alumni, will enable a more complete view. These data points can be tied together to create one cohesive story about the student."[23]

Pelletier makes a compelling point about data disaggregation. "When data is not disaggregated, there is the potential to reinforce bias or to wash out differences between groups—thus missing opportunities to improve programs, services, and support and to better understand the context and story of those particular students," she notes in the *EDUCAUSE Review* article.

The power of data use can be compelling, particularly when shared, so there is an understanding by stakeholders as to the what and the why, which are essential. In the book *Good to Great*, Jim Collins writes, "The beauty and power of the research finding is that they can radically simplify our lives while increasing our effectiveness. There is great solace in the simple fact of clarity—about what is vital, and what is not" (p. 205). Coupled with an understanding of what it means to find your Hedgehog concept (p. 90), higher education institutions can devise a more targeted approach and vision to retain and help students succeed. The Hedgehog Concept, developed by Jim Collins, as described in the book *Good to Great*, enables organizations to assess their goal or passion based on their mission, determine what they do best, and identify what its economic engine is. Where those three areas intersect is the sweet spot that can guide strategy to expand, scale up, update, or make improvements.

Meaningful collaboration can build on individual strengths within an institution that can ultimately support the strategic aims and needs of the institution. Recognizing that not everything can be accomplished in-house, and consultants and/or services may need to be outsourced, collaboration can mean having departments that report to different areas of the college work together as they maximize internal expertise toward achieving a goal. For example, connecting individuals who have student information systems, enterprise, and learning management expertise with IT, enrollment, and/or student affairs. This internal partnership can be used to develop reports or augment systems that are relevant to the college and allow stakeholders to turn data into relevant information they can use to inform decisions. Cheryl Hyman, author of *Reinvention*, summarizes, "Collaboration does not always equal consensus, and decision making by leaders does not always equal autocracy" (2018 p. 140).

GROUP WORK TOWARD "COOPERTITION"

Competition between faculty and staff, administration and faculty, and externally with colleges and universities will never end yet can be tempered. Given the current state of higher education, perhaps more can be done in "coopertition," term coined by authors of *Wired for Success*, Aldridge and Harvatt. Emerged from combining the words "cooperation" and "competition," "coopertition" suggests "teaming up to expand competitive advantage."[24] According to *Wired for Success*, this blended mindset of healthy competition and cooperation enables institutions to "pool precious resources, provide better academic programs, test-drive expensive new technologies and exchange valuable information about students success strategies."

Pelletier advises that "keeping the student first in strategic and tactical decisions can encourage all departments to be laser-focused on one priority.... Academic advising staff and technologies can serve as a key lever for outreach and resource delivery. In fact, cross-institutional collaboration is critical to moving student success efforts forward, and one department alone cannot carry the full weight."[25]

According to Daniel Coyle, author of *The Culture Code*, "building habits of group vulnerability is link building a muscle. It takes time, repetition, and the willingness to feel pain in order to feel gains" (p. 158). In light of challenges, working together is imperative. It is the only way, as leadership cannot do it alone. Facing and embracing the vulnerability of needing to work collaboratively shows strength and gets to move the rest of the players to feel comfortable sharing their insecurities, disarming the company to feel comfortable for truth telling and work.

In her book *Reinvention* (2018), Hyman writes about the system-wide calls to action made in the City Colleges of Chicago to improve student success when she was its chancellor. The reform program was called Reinvention. "Just as we needed to invest in student supports, we needed to invest in our own employees, which are the fuel of the institution.... Everything we did was supported by collaborative efforts with our employees. The objective was as shared commitment to student success" (p. 57). This reform program's eight task forces tackled faculty and staff, development, succession planning, operations optimization, financial sustainability, and more. The financial piece of steering the future of higher education is critical and, as mentioned in other sections, also calls for visionary, transparent, and actionable stewardship. In the article *The Modern CFO: Adapting to a Time of Crisis*, Shaun Taylor writes, "While stewardship of the health of the balance sheet remains as important as ever, the modern CFP will communicate and collaborate with other areas of the business to foster shared ownership of costs and delivery."[26]

As institutions look to secure more revenue and funds to support endeavors, Hyman suggests in her book that, of course, it helps, but an infusion of funds may not be the answer if other more important things are not in place. During her tenure, she instead focused on how funds were being utilized at City Colleges of Chicago and "determined not to solicit or accept money from outside sources until I know we had our financial house in order and could spend any new money efficiently on revamped programs and capital investments" (p. 54).

This is an important recommendation and point of reflection. During more fluid times, institutions that are now most affected benefited from rolling enrollment and tuition revenue, and did not consider the possibility of more urgent times in the future and what to do if and when. As most institutions have been and are continuing to look at enrollment "like stockbrokers during a crash," Hyman explains in her book the importance of focusing on completion, moving from a focus on success indicators "simply by counting chairs (and the funding that accompanied them) to one focused on both access and success . . . enrollment for the sake of enrollment can cause one to lose focus on the importance of on-time completion" (pp. 126–127).

ABOUT RESISTANCE AND THE NEED FOR SHARED GOVERNANCE

To work toward change, shared governance in its true sense represents where all parties are consulted, all parties deliberate, debate, plan, find consensus, and move forward with actionable next steps. "Even when you know your cause is just, there comes a time when you can't face the resistance alone," underscores Hyman, author of *Reinvention* (2018). Leadership needs to recognize too that sometimes politics "trumps performance" (p. 137).

In her book, Hyman articulates on the resistance that *Reinvention* experienced in Illinois that may also resonate and help others trying to reinvent or revision for the good of student success:

> To the faculty who continually opposed Reinvention, though it felt to me that it was not about sharing at all, but rather that administrators were supposed to have very limited input on all things academic, whereas faculty, would have a say on all administrative matters. Of course, that's unrealistic: such an arrangement would fail to provide the balance or benefits the institution needed to achieve sustainable change. (p. 140)

For example, most recently during the coronavirus, colleges have their "feet" to the fire as they have had to make immediate decisions about how to seamlessly transition in-class instruction online and also keep operations running smoothly. Specifically, with nationwide stay-at-home mandates to enforce social distancing in an effort to flatten the virus uptick, campus leaders have had to consider how to effectively communicate with faculty students and the community. Decisions about how to orchestrate admissions, placement testing, online proctoring, enrollment, registration, campus services, IT support, student resources, and course scheduling for future semesters involve convenings and sometimes difficult conversations among stakeholders. While many should weigh in and provide insight, who decides? Recognizing the important role of shared governance, what falls under the purview of administration or faculty or both? Whose role is it to make the ultimate decision? And in making decisions, what should consensus look like?

Progress can be made when multifarious groups listen and dialogue appreciatively. Angela Provitera McGlynn discussed in her book *Successful Beginnings for College Teaching* how students tell faculty what they want. And while retention literature points to having a sense of belonging as a key factor in retaining students, cues to learning how to create that atmosphere of community[27] in the classroom and on campus come directly from students, if stakeholders are listening. "Clearly, our students are telling us how to create a safe environment and giving us tips on how to build rapport with them" (p. 64).

Examination of a pathways approach as a model that supports student success attainment, the authors of *Redesigning America's Community College* discuss the lack of relational trust (Bryk and Schneider, 2003) and how "fragmented" shared governance limits progress. "As part of this process, faculty must move from a reactive to a proactive stance, and the administration will need to encourage and support this move" (Bailey, Jaggars, & Jenkins, 2015, p. 145).

While shared governance discourages the *us-versus-them* approach, among leaders it can also entail a transformation from *I to we*, which can be helpful in advancing change through collaborative and cooperative work. To this point, in his book *Discovering Your Truth North*, Bill George writes about the value in learning to share power. An example was how Steve Jobs changed after being fired from Apple, realizing "he didn't have to do everything by himself . . . learned how to nurture great teams and recognize their contributions" (p. 191). Similarly, George features Whole Foods cofounder John Mackey, who modified his leadership style at a time Whole Foods sales declined and stock price dropped in 2008. Mackey was faced with the realization that it was time to consider other perspectives and ways of moving the business forward. He alone did not have the answer, nor could he do it alone (p. 193).

Exploring change through shared governance and multivariate cognitive lenses, organizations can survive the growing pains of necessary transformative processes. A realization, however, is that while shared governance is a noble start, an imbalance of empowerment and authority can slow the process. And when groups deliberating are on the same playing field, then communication can also possibly reach a stalemate. In *Reframing Organizations*, Lee Bolman and Terrence Deal cite from Machiavelli's *The Prince*:

> It must be realized that there is nothing more difficult to plan, more uncertain success, or more dangerous to manage than the establishment of a new order of [things]; for he who introduces [change] makes enemies of all those who derived advantage from the old order and finds but lukewarm defenders among those who stand to gain from the new one. (1514 1961, p. 27) (p. 378)

The impasse observed in higher education not only stems between different contractual groups but also, and not surprisingly, from within leadership, particularly when organization structures are modified and there is a combination of new and long-standing employees.

Bolman and Deal conclude, "Organizational change . . . rarely works to retrain people without revising roles, or to revamp roles without retraining. Planning without broad-based participation...almost guarantees stiff resistance later on. Change alters power relationships and undermine existing agreements and pacts" (p. 378). For example, the recent emergency transition to remote teaching has been fueled by need, and not by administrative recommendation alone, which has earned change more traction. Under normal circumstances, contention would be the outcome of some conversations concerning proposed new or streamlined academic programs, course offerings, online course design, and development as well as the adoption of technology for instruction or support, such as predictive analytics and advising and student retention alert systems. According to Gail Mellow and Cynthia Heelan authors of *Minding the Dream: The Process and Practice of the American Community College*, "This view of administration as an oppositional force to faculty concerns emerges from multiple and long-standing traditions on some campuses, and is inflamed by old-fashioned unions on the one side, and faculty bashing administrators on the other" (p. 146).

In describing the kind of leadership necessary to move past disagreements that pale in comparison to the larger issues facing the entire college community, Mellow and Heelan highlight the following:

> The ideal leader has vision and makes expert use of data from the field and builds a team that can implement the necessary foundation to achieve the dream . . . making education success a reality for the many people who otherwise would never have the opportunity to attend college and for the many who still

experience a community college as a revolving door . . . they celebrate grades of every age and cultural group and they enjoy the collegiality of true partnership in their communities. (p. 134)

Stewardship that builds relational trust makes a difference. A way to build or reinforce relational trust is through "professional competence, personal integrity, and collegial respect. Leaders need to realize the importance of publicly displaying the latter two of these" (Bailey, Jaggars, & Jenkins, 2015, p. 147).

BACK TO BUSINESS

What education can learn from business should be welcomed in order to gain a broader perspective. The use of resource-sharing, alliances, and outsourcing as well as consortium pricing for a variety services are among the many approaches that can be modeled and suited to higher education. Other strategies include: stakeholder marketing and strategic financial planning that can help institutions create multiyear strategically driven plans.[28]

In a case study conducted by Ahi Sibel, *Applying Business Models to Higher Education*,

the researcher uses the Malcolm Baldrige National Quality Award Criteria (MBNQAC) to understand core values and the concepts of those seven criteria which are:

1) leadership
2) strategic planning
3) student, stakeholder and market focus
4) measurement, analysis, and knowledge management
5) faculty and staff focus
6) process management and
7) organizational performance results.

These criteria are analyzed with visionary leadership and a comparison of the strategic plans of Alvernia University and Kutztown University. The changes imperative for higher education institutions include the redesign of education, more flexible faculty, increased efficiency, removal of boundaries, and entry into new markets. In addition, challenges and conflicts facing the change process are also discussed in the context of Kotter's Change Theory."[29]

Review of successful for-profits and institutions that integrate business insights and take a business approach to higher education management can be helpful in operating higher education institutions more efficiently. *Proceedings of the International Conference on Business Excellence* in March 2020 noted:

> Excellence models have been used successfully also in business education. Business education reflects the added value to sound economic development, balancing social and economic interest (Emiliani, 2004). In general, it refers to competitive and motivated academic staff, quality of teaching and learning activities, leadership and management commitment, sustainability of university-business relationship, internationalization strategy and comprehensive curriculum adapted to business environment.[30]

John Harney published in the *New England Journal of Higher Education*: "Even today, elements of business models, including differences in institutional control, segment and mission, are not widely appreciated in higher ed. But there's a perceived need for a common vocabulary and analytical framework to support dialog among diverse stakeholders including students, faculty, staff, administrators and trustees."

The 2020 EDUCAUSE Horizon Report—Teaching and Learning Edition—reinforces the notion that "institutions need to demonstrate their value and/or adjust to economic realities with new business and funding models"[31] such as the sustainable use of OER adoption and alternate education pathways such as nano and micro degrees, stackable credentials, and partnerships.

As Catalogue for Philanthropy founder George McCully noted in a recent NEJHE (New England Board of Higher Education) forum: "The business model is a major challenge for higher ed. At the same time, major institutions which have very large endowments are in a positive feedback loop that is intrinsically inefficient. Harvard earns more from the yield on its endowment in a single year than its development officers can raise in five years" (Harney, 2013).

Issues presented at the October 2013 Summit of Cost iterate issues to date:

- "Student persistence and retention are the largest levers and most promising tools for increasing institutional productivity and for improving the financial bottomline. Over half of institutions have graduation rates under 50%—which represents a significant loss of resources given the time and money they spend recruiting and onboarding students. Most HEIs need to consider hiring a chief retention officer if they haven't already."[32]
- "HEIs cannot 'cut' their way to success or profitability (by simply reducing costs), or 'revenue' their way to success (by finding additional revenue sources). Cost equations must change, because revenue equation is not going to change favorably. Revenues will be hard to come by, as Pell Grants

will not grow and students will be needier. Thus, a fundamental reconsideration of business models is necessary."³³

Despite anecdotal and concrete examples of success, it has not been uncommon for consideration of business and leadership strategies and practices to receive a lukewarm reception by some in education. For example, the application of Kotter's eight-step Process for Leading Change has been challenged as steps suitable for organizational change. "We still regularly hear questions and comments like, 'Does this really work in education?' and 'You normally work in the private sector—we are different'" (Akhtar & Kotter, 2019). But it can and is grounded in principles that promote and encourage buy-in for change from the "heart."³⁴ While the journey toward change in any industry is not exactly linear, the thought of a pathway or steps may be resisted. Nevertheless, the advice presented suggests a process that might help organizations move through difficult conversations favoring common goal.

In striving toward ensuring student success, the use of encouraging and motivational terms is repeatedly found in dialogue about aspirational goals in this space that discuss the desire to support, retain, and graduate students. However, the synergy needed to move away from what Aktar and Kotter (2019) call "only Have To and create Want To/Get To" requires more than well-intentioned lip service, buzzwords, and semantics. This transformation urges diverse action, action calls for change, and sustainable change summons courage to face objections and collaboration.

To that end, pages from the penguin story *Our Iceberg Is Melting* (2005) bring to life characters (the NoNo, the Alices and Freds,), attitudes, a relatable urgent scenario about what to do, lessons and possibilities for change that can be applied (like business models) across industries, and more importantly higher education. The Cast of Penguins, which represents all–too-familiar characters in reality, is as follows:

- Fred—curious and creative
- Alice—action oriented, part of leadership
- Louis—head leader
- Buddy—compassionate, likable and trustworthy
- The Professor—the intellectual some find annoying
- NoNo—always resistant to change

In facing their dilemma, Kotter and Rathgeber reflect about the penguin colony: "the most remarkable change of all was in how so many members of the colony had grown less afraid of change, were learning the specific steps need to make any large adjustment to new circumstances and worked well together to keep leaping into a better and better future" (p. 123). Examining the challenges in higher education and the need to support the diverse needs of students combined with the additional societal and economic stressors affecting both students and institutions, the lessons highlighted in Kotter's and Rathgeber's fictional story offer insight about how to address organizational and interpersonal struggles.

The use of questions is also useful in exploring change, smoothing over difficulties, and fostering relationships critical to higher education. Building trust and gaining respect do not happen just by saying it will or by willing it, particularly in a space where various interest groups (students, faculty, administrators, staff) converge. Mindful, purposeful, deliberate questions conceive productive discourse, which is helpful when troubleshooting, brainstorming, or addressing and traversing controversial or unknown territory. Inquisitively and innocently, children do it so well. Exiting adolescence and coming into adulthood, some individuals retire the ability to use questions to an advantage that contributes to productive, collaborative, and engaging work environments. Warren Berger, author of *The Book of Beautiful Questions*, says kids realize questions give them insight but are also excellent ice breakers. If they can do it, everyone should or could learn to do it too. Berger dedicates a chapter to questions that help connect with others "designed to strength relationships old and new" (p. 106).

Suggestions provided by Berger include the following:

- Ask authentic questions.
- Try to suspend judgment.
- Withhold advice (focus more in inquiry).
- Ask open-ended questions.
- Be willing to listen carefully.
- Follow up on answers.

Some questions from the *Book of Beautiful Questions* that can help divisive situations are as follows (p. 132)"

- What is it in your position that gives you pause?
- Can we imagine a position that might at least partly satisfy us?
- How might we form a stronger partnership?

Whether people are questioning up, down, or across professional levels, Berger notes that individuals regardless of title or position should be mindful and "frame a question to indicate that you're open to change" (p. 140). "Questions serve as connectors" and "can also help us bring those people together and rally them around a larger mission and shared sense of purpose," he writes. In higher education, working on cross-functional efforts to tackle institutional goals and challenges raises questions such as who owns the project, who will ultimately be responsible, who will be held responsible, how to hold individuals accountable to ensure project completion, and so on. The current strain in enrollment presents the big task from departments or divisions directly responsible for enrollment for collaboration from other areas. The reality is that whether or not a department's functional role is directly or indirectly involved in enrollment, everyone's contribution has a direct impact. The stay-in-your-lane mindset is not an easy perspective to shift, but questions are as follows:

- How can operational areas work toward a common goal?
- How can teams work collaboratively without the specter of territorialism?
- How can co-leading work?
- How can mutual respect and recognition of faculty-administration roles in higher education be achieved, supported, nurtured?
- What are elements of student success-centered employee (administrative and faculty) contracts?
- What are you afraid of?
- What about working with (department X, your colleague) concern you?

Potts and LaMarsh elaborate in *Master Change, Maximize Success* that communication, listening, and requesting feedback and reacting to feedback are important. "Ensuring that everyone feels like partners in a two-way communication process will go a long way toward gaining commitment to the change" (p. 118). Building trust may sound cliché in organizational environments where politics is a natural inevitability; however, trust is real concern as it is important in fostering productive working relationships. While in some cases there may be legitimate reasons for a lack of trust, other times, resistance surfaces when individuals fear being outshined, overlooked, undermined, excluded, outperformed, and the like. To follow a simple question can emerge: why? If the answer to that question points to irrational insecurities grounded in plain territorialism, rank, and/or underperformance, think about how that can impact institutional progress.

Questions can help serve as a primer to meetings and change. Without questions, perspectives can be missed and people can find themselves in a "homogenous bubble" that negates or sees no need to change. Berger quotes Roselinde Torres "that being in a bubble can limit the leaders ability to anticipate change . . . having that diverse network helps in identify trends and cultural patters, so every leader must ask, Am I bringing together diverse people who can share points of view that I might be missing?" (p. 161). The act of gathering diverse networks can contribute to expanded perspectives and also lend clarity, streamline, and minimize duplication of efforts. Consider student outreach and communication, and how confusing it might be for students toggle between communication systems and college calendars to learn about events on campus, important dates, campus updates, resources, support services, hours of operations, faculty office hours, and so on. Consider how communication might improve between administration and faculty for sharing technology and policy updates, scheduling events, and meetings.

Mellow and Heelan, authors of *Minding the Dream: the Process and practice of the American Community College*, wrote: "Ideally the entire college campus has a role in sustaining and improving student learning. Incredible learning can result with faculty work together with student support staff to create a total focus on learning, knowing, and doing within the institution" (p. 102).

Without students, higher education would be an empty space. Ultimately, the goal of all efforts should support the student. Walter Bumphus, president and CEO of American Association of Community Colleges, noted in an AACC webinar "Prepare to Open: Strategies for Reengaging Students, Faculty, Staff, and Community After COVID-19": "Students do not come to us as FTE. They come to us as students and as individuals," and so institutions must work to identify how best they can support students to get them to where they want and need to go.

Setting aside inconsequential differences, higher education must address the developing needs of students to ensure their success and this industry's survival. Integrated into the services provided, there should be consideration about multiple intelligences, emotional intelligences, as well as a more extensive look at reasonable accommodations for students as well as staff.

During COVID-19 the move to online has impacted decisions about course design, delivery, instructional modality, equity and access for staff, student and faculty, and how best to carry out these obligations. Suddenly online education is not a topic for discussion but the only option. However, as institutions huddle to develop ways to meet student needs and continue instruction without interruption, viable options and solutions have emerged from creative thinking about the transformative opportunities that online instruction provides during the during the crisis and after. It is during this process that higher education can remind audiences of its value despite dismissive remarks to the contrary.

In an article entitled "Georgia Tech Scientist: Life's Not Going to Snap Back to Normal so Let's Improve Remote Learning, author Maureen Downey talks about revisioning online instruction: "where we can think bigger and better—blending remote and in-person learning to increase access to education while still providing the kind of college and classroom experience students want (and need)."

In the article she quotes David Joyner, a senior research associate in the Georgia Tech College of Computing and executive director of Tech's online Master of Science in Computer Science program guest column, on pushing the boundaries of online instructional delivery:

> Once you've broken down the sanctity of the synchronous, collocated classroom, other barriers start to collapse. Dual enrollment, where high school students enroll in college classes, becomes significantly easier: those students become part of an online cohort of students. Adult learners, students with certain disabilities, international students: all encounter major barriers from geography, synchronicity, and cost. Removing physical location as a constraint immediately improves accessibility for those students.[35]

During the COVID-19 debacle and just a few months before the 2020 presidential election, the Trump White House urges unemployed people to find something new. "This initiative is about challenging the idea the traditional 2 and 4 yr college is the only option to acquire the skills needed to secure a job."[36] A mild threat to higher education, this is not a first. In 2019 the IBM Institute for Business Ventures announced the results of its study that "120 million people worldwide will need" retraining "to be ready to work with automation and AI." In the article "The Workforce Is Calling, Higher Education, Will You Answer?," Heather E. McGowan asks the question citing if the 20 million undergraduates will be ready for the marketplace. McGowan categorically writes: "American universities are in crisis with their very business model and value proposition under threat. Yet they miss the elephant in the room; if you consider the urgent need to retrain the U.S. workforce, there is unmet market demand to serve a population more than half the size of the current undergraduate classes."[37]

On the heels of the White House statement and the challenges of the pandemic and unemployment sitting at 11.1 percent[38] in June 2020 according to the Bureau of Labor Statistics, colleges are called to task to continue being student-ready pillars of opportunity. As higher education presents itself as an option for all, the student profile is as diverse as ever. Dual enrollment students in high school, adult learners, international students, students with disabilities are part of the make-up of learners today and institutions are learning how best to reach and support them all considering companion technologies in a strategic, deliberate, and universal approach.

The use of virtual chatbots have potential as recruitment and communication tools and also serve students with disabilities. AI-powered systems also help institutions expand student support services by extending hours of operations. According to the National Center for Education Statistics, 19 percent of undergraduates in 2015–16 reported having a disability.[39] While COVID-19 has magnified the issues this student demographic grapples with, a recent study shows the challenges aren't exactly new.[40]

Haben Girma, author of *Haben: the Deafblind Woman Who Conquered Harvard Law*, cites there are over 57 million Americans with disabilities. Her undergraduate experiences at Lewis and Clarke and at Harvard Law are testament to institutions that were determined to listen and support students. As the first braille reader at Lewis & Clarke College, Haben Girma's undergraduate experience demonstrates the determination and commitment of Lewis & Clarke College as an example to others that yes they can: "They purchased a braille embosser, purchased braille translation software, and then spent the summer learning how to produce brail. They're not afraid of the unknown; they learn, explore, and discover for the sake of their students and the betterment of themselves."[41]

Laura Rothstein wrote about this issue in 1991 in *Campuses and the Disabled*, in which she discussed how campuses were investing millions of dollars to make campus building accessible for disabled students, professors, and staff to serve this population and stay in compliance since Section 504 of the Rehabilitation Act of 1973, and later, the Americans with Disabilities Act, was passed in 1990. "The institution must make reasonable accommodations such as allowing reduced course loads, extra time for exams, or the tape-recording of classes, as long as such activities do not fundamentally alter the program or create an undue administrative or financial burden on the institution. In addition, the Rehabilitation Act requires architectural accessibility for disabled students. While not every single classroom need be accessible, the educational program as a whole should be" (Grigely, 2017).

Girma delivered a speech at the White House's 25th anniversary of the American with Disabilities Act during the Barack Obama administration: "In 2010, I entered Harvard Law School as its first Deaf-blind student. Harvard didn't know exactly how a Deafblind student would succeed. And honestly, I didn't know how I would survive. Without having all the answers, we pioneered our way using assistive technology and high expectations" (pp. 254–55). That was a decade ago and unsung pioneers existed to advance student success of students with disabilities. With enhancements in assistive technology, mediated communication, and the development of accessibility software, there is excuse for limited support for these students. An approach that is inclusive and supports universal design for learning makes education and instructional accessible for all.

It is necessary to come to terms that the higher education population is changing, and so must the work to support it. Dr. Ohrablo recommends in *High Impact Advising*, "Each student is unique in his or her experience. If we generalize a student's issue and develop a recommended plan of action without proper assessment, we run the risk of missing the mark in terms of providing appropriate support" (p.38).

In *Master Change, Maximize Success*, the authors discuss how reaching the "desired state" several things are at work and need to be considered: "structure, processes, people and culture" (p. 42).

In that vein, it is a duty to leaven the future by way of thoughtful and intentional and actionable communication that aim to advance improvements for a better tomorrow. Potts and LaMarsh explain that in seeking to reach the desired state which consists of structure, processes, people, and culture, it is crucial to realize that "change is one is probably going to have an impact on the other" (p. 42).

Stakeholders should deliberate and advocate necessary change grounded in the reality of the existing tensions and challenges of the institutions. "With strategic thought, inspired collaboration, research-driven models, and carefully selected technologies, we can indeed 'wire' our students, as well as our institutions, for success now and in the future," writes Dr. Aldridge.

In an article, *The Gift of Goodbye: Saying Goodbye to Normal and Hello to Extraordinary*, Shai Butler notes: "Old ideas, old approaches, old pedagogy, old polices, old instructional techniques, old co-curricular programming models, old biases, all of the old sacred cows that we were committed to sustaining even though they stopped working for the benefit of the institution and our students long ago. We have found ourselves thrust into a 'change or die' paradigm. To not have acted promptly would have made us appear tone-deaf to the urgency of now, and out of touch with the circumstances that we find ourselves in as a profession."[42] At a new juncture, higher education, aware of the numbers dwindling in the classroom, is compelled to make sense of its new precarious situation that has been exacerbated precipitously by the pandemic.

Dr. Joianne Smith, Oakton Community College's president, recalls in a 2018 article in *Inside Higher ED*, the volume of students who were exiting the college per day in 2015 motivated the launch of the All for One program (that asked faculty and staff members to reach out to at least one student at least five times a semester), which subsequently led to the faculty's support effort—the Persistence Project. "We have heard hundreds of stories from our faculty about why this works so well," Graff said. "It's because this project emphasizes human connection. If a student makes that connection, the student is more likely to persist, but it also makes us better teachers" (Hollace Graff, a philosophy professor who chairs Oakton's humanities and philosophy department and who led the Persistence Project.)[43]

Creative faculty and staff support, collaborative work, inclusive student-centered practices complemented by AI and Machine Learning can make a difference in college operations, the future of learning, teaching, recruitment, retention, and student success. The 2020 EDUCAUSE Horizon report cites the positive application of artificial intelligence at the University of Oklahoma: To date, more than 28,000 student interactions have been logged using SoonerBot, [an automated chatbot] contributing, at least in part, to the largest freshman class in OU's history in fall 2019." While not everyone may be on board due to prohibitive cost or time required to develop in-house, a scan of college websites around the country shows an increase in the use of AI. "Although developing a chatbot can involve a significant time and resource investment that requires specialized development, that investment might yield returns in the form of extended hours and operation of the university to meet the needs of a 24/7/365 audience."[44]

The idea a backlog of students who would have returned to college or registered for the first time if institutions had had the foresight to address their needs is a gamble higher education should not make. Why wait until then? Who will fill class seats on-campus or virtually? What enrollment trends will look like in the future? Changing. Speculative. Up for interpretation. The present uncertainties on the education horizon should be the driver to work collaboratively now so prospective and current students of all ages continue to opt for the value education, and institutions can listen, learn, engage, and support them toward success like never before—one cohort at a time.

NOTES

1. Soria, Krista M., and Robin Stubblefield. "Building a Strengths-Based Campus to Support Student Retention." *Journal of College Student Development* 56, no. 6 (2015): 626–631. doi:10.1353/csd.2015.0056.

2. Tinto, Vincent (2006). Research and Practice of Student Retention: What Next?. *Journal of College Student Retention: Research, Theory and Practice* 8: 1–19. doi:10.2190/C0C4-EFT9-EG7W-PWP4.

3. Shea Smith, K. (2013, July 26). The Inner Student: Kathleen Shea Smith at TEDxFSU. Retrieved from https://www.youtube.com/watch?v=meQSpp3YO9o.

4. Ma, J., Pender, M., and Welch, M. (2019). Education Pays 2019: The Benefits of Higher Education for Individuals and Society. Trends in Higher Education Series. The College Board. Retrieved from https://research.collegeboard.org/pdf/education-pays-2019-full-report.pdf.

5. The RP Group. The Research & Planning Group for California Community Colleges.
    Understanding the Student Experience through the Loss/Momentum Framework:
    Clearing the Path to Completion. Retrieved from http://ncii-improve.com/wp-content/uploads/2017/06/CbD-Understanding.pdf.

6. Soares, Louis, Patricia Steele, and Lindsay Wayt (2016). *Evolving Higher Education Business Models: Leading with Data to Deliver Results.* Washington, DC: American Council on Education. https://www.acenet.edu/Documents/Evolving-Higher-Education-Business-Models.pdf.

7. Matson, T., and Robinson, J. (2018, April 5). Using a Strengths-Based Approach to Retain College Students. GALLUP. Retrieved from https://www.gallup.com/workplace/236063/using-strengths-based-approach-retain-college-students.aspx.

8. St. Armour, M. (2019, October 21). Marketing Firm Breaks Down Personas of Adult Learners to Help Colleges Recruit Better. Inside Higher Ed. Retrieved from https://www.insidehighered.com/print/news/2019/10/21/marketing-firm-breaks-down-personas-adult-learners-help-colleges-recruit-better.

9. National Student Clearinghouse Research Center (Fall 2019). Current Term Enrollment Estimates Fall 2019. Retrieved from https://nscresearchcenter.org/wp-content/uploads/CTEE_Report_Fall_2019.pdf.

10. Mitchell, T. (2019, March 11). Changing Demographics and Digital Transformation. EDUCAUSE. Retrieved from https://er.educause.edu/-/media/files/articles/2019/3/er191101.pdf.

Mitchell, T. (2019, March 11). Changing Demographics and Digital Transformation. EDUCAUSE. Retrieved from https://er.educause.edu/-/media/files/articles/2019/3/er191101.pdf.

11. Center for Community College Student Engagement (2018). Show Me the Way: The Power of Advising Community Colleges.

12. *What Really Works: A Review of Student Success Initiatives.* Civitas. Retrieved from https://www.civitaslearning.com/research/.

13. Ellucian CRM. *Evolving Early Alerts Early Engagement.* Retrieved from https://www.ellucian.com/assets/en/white-paper/whitepaper-evolving-early-alerts-early-engagement.pdf.

14. Centers for Disease Control and Prevention. Coronavirus Disease 2019 (COVID-19). Cases in the U.S. Retrieved from https://www.cdc.gov/coronavirus/2019-ncov/cases-updates/cases-in-us.html.

15. Soares, Louis, Patricia Steele, and Lindsay Wayt. 2016. *Evolving Higher Education Business Models: Leading with Data to Deliver Results.* Washington, DC: American Council on Education.

16. The Chronicle of Higher Education. As Covid-19 Pummels Budgets, Colleges Are Resorting to Layoffs and Furloughs. Here's the Latest (updated 2020, July 2). Retrieved from https://www.chronicle.com/article/as-covid-19-pummels-budgets/248779?cid=wcontentgrid_hp_2.

17. Nietzel, Michael T. (2020, July 1). June Brought More Faculty Layoffs and Growing Pushback. Forbes. Retrieved from https://www.forbes.com/sites/michaeltnietzel/2020/07/01/june-brought-more-layoffs-and-growing-faculty-pushback/#54879cf4fcae.

18. Adams, L. (2020, June 22). Dozens of Christian College Faculty Eliminated in Spring Budget Cuts. Christianity Today. Retrieved from https://www.christia

nitytoday.com/news/2020/june/christian-college-cuts-bethel-harding-john-brown-cccu.html.

19. McKenzie, L. (2020, July 17). Rethinking the Pennsylvania State System. Inside Higher ED. Retrieved from https://www.insidehighered.com/news/2020/07/17/pennsylvania-university-system-proposes-plan-redesign?utm_source=Inside+Higher+Ed&utm_campaign=ee77ae3507-DNU_2020_COPY_02&utm_medium=email&utm_term=0_1fcbc04421-ee77ae3507-236299941&mc_cid=ee77ae3507&mc_eid=89c7107097.

20. StrataEducation.org (2019, November 18). Changing the Value of Education. Retrieved from https://www.stradaeducation.org/report/changing-the-value-equation-for-higher-education/.

21. True Value: A New Model for Measuring the Value of Postsecondary Education by Listening to Americans: Survey of 340,000 Adults Informs Creation of Strada Education Consumer Value Equation, Providing New Insight into Learners' Needs and Priorities. 2019. PR Newswire, Nov 18. Retrieved from http://libdb.dccc.edu/login?url=https://search.proquest.com/docview/2315049290?accountid=10459.

22. StrataEducation.org. Changing the Value of Education. Retrieved from https://www.stradaeducation.org/report/changing-the-value-equation-for-higher-education/.

23. Pelletier, Kathe (2019, October 14). Student Success: 3 Big Questions. Educause Review. Retrieved from https://er.educause.edu/articles/2019/10/student-success--3-big-questions.

24. Aldridge, S., and Harvatt, K. (2014). *Wired for Success: Real World Solutions for Transforming Higher Education.* New York: American Association of State Colleges and Universities.

25. Pelletier, Kathe (2019, October 14). Student Success: 3 Big Questions. Educause Review. Retrieved from https://er.educause.edu/articles/2019/10/student-success--3-big-questions.

26. Taylor, Shaun (2020, July). The Modern CFO: Adapting to a Time of Crisis. Strategic Finance. (pp. 42–47).

27. McGlynn, Angela Provitera (2001). *Successful Beginnings for College Teaching.* Atwood Publishing. Madison, WI.

28. Kaufman Hall Unveils Strategic Financial Planning Maturity Model for Higher Education at NACUBO Annual Meeting: New Model Gives Educational Institutions the Ability to Better Assess Their Progress in Building a Mature and Successful Financial Planning Process, and Create a Roadmap for Improvement. 2019. PR Newswire, Jul 15.

29. Sibel Ahi. "Applying Business Models to Higher Education." *International Journal of Educational Administration and Policy Studies* 10, no. 9 (2018): 111–122.

30. Dima, Alina Mihaela, Roxana Clodnițchi, Laura Istudor, et al. (2019). Business Excellence Models in Higher Education—Innovative Solutions for Management Performance. *Proceedings of the International Conference on Business Excellence* 13(1): 38–46. Retrieved 9 Mar. 2020, from doi:10.2478/picbe-2019-0005.

31. 2020 EDUCAUSE Horizon Report. Teaching and Learning Edition. https://library.educause.edu/resources/2020/3/2020-educause-horizon-report-teaching-and-learning-edition.

32. Davis Educational Foundation. Summon on Cost in Higher Education October 20–21, 2013. Retrieved from http://www.nebhe.org/info/pdf/events/conference/october2013/SCHE_Key_Themes.pdf.

33. Davis Educational Foundation. Summon on Cost in Higher Education October 20–21, 2013. Retrieved from http://www.nebhe.org/info/pdf/events/conference/october2013/SCHE_Key_Themes.pdf.

34. Akhtar, Vanessa Loverme, and Kotter, John P. (2019). Charting the Course—the Path to Transformation in Education. Retrieved from https://www.kotterinc.com/wp-content/uploads/2019/03/Transformation-in-Education-web-version.pdf.

35. Downey, Maureen (2020, July 14). Georgia Tech Scientist: Life's Not Going to Snap Back to Normal so Let's Improve Remote Learning. The Atlanta Journal-Constitution. https://www.ajc.com/blog/get-schooled/georgia-tech-scientist-life-not-going-snap-back-normal-let-improve-remote-learning/DwogtXA9hMEqgNWEEmiGmL/.

36. Shaban, Hamza (2020, July 14). White House Tells 18 Million Unemployed Workers to "Find Something New" in Ad Campaign. The Washington Post. https://www.washingtonpost.com/business/2020/07/14/ivanka-trump-jobs-find-something-new/.

37. McGowan, Heather E. (2019, September 10). The Workforce Is Calling, Higher Education, Will You Answer?" Forbes. Retrieved from https://www.forbes.com/sites/heathermcgowan/2019/09/10/the-workforce-is-calling-higher-education-will-you-answer/#5a83e3276f6f.

38. Bureau of Labor Statistics. The Employment Situation—June 2020. Retrieved from https://www.bls.gov/news.release/pdf/empsit.pdf.

39. National Center for Education Statistics. Students with Disabilities. Retrieved from https://nces.ed.gov/fastfacts/display.asp?id=60.

40. Gierdowski, D. and Galanek, J. (2020, June 1). ECAR Study of the Technology Needs of Students with Disabilities, 2020. EDUCAUSE Review. Retrieved from https://er.educause.edu/blogs/2020/6/ecar-study-of-the-technology-needs-of-students-with-disabilities-2020.

41. Girma, Haben. (2019). *Haben: The Deafblind Woman Who Conquered Harvard Law*. New York: Twelve.

42. Butler, Shai L (2020, April 20). The Gift of Goodbye: Saying Goodbye to Normal and Hello to Extraordinary. Retrieved from https://www.higheredjobs.com/articles/articleDisplay.cfm?ID=2209&utm_source=04_20_2020&utm_medium=email&utm_campaign=ExecutiveInsiderUpdat.

43. Smith, Ashley A. (2018, March 13). The Persistence Project. Inside Higher ED. Retrieved from https://www.insidehighered.com/news/2018/03/13/oakton-community-college-builds-faculty-student-relationships-increase-persistence.

44. 2020 EDUCAUSE Horizon Report. Teaching and Learning Edition https://library.educause.edu/resources/2020/3/2020-educause-horizon-report-teaching-and-learning-edition.

Education Resource Guide

The following organizations support student success advocacy and serve as an information repository and network for higher education professionals.

Association of International Education Administrators (AIEA): "A member organization that equips leaders to shape the future of higher education in a global context." https://www.aieaworld.org/

American Association of Community Colleges: "Represents and advocates for nearly 1,200 associate-degree-granting institutions enrolling more than 12 million students—almost half of all U.S. undergraduates." https://www.aacc.nche.edu/about-us/

American Educational Research Association (AERA): "A national research society, strives to advance knowledge about education, to encourage scholarly inquiry related to education, and to promote the use of research to improve education and serve the public good." https://www.aera.net/

American Association for Higher Education: "Its members are faculty, administrators, and students.... Through its members, AAHEA promotes effective change at the campus, state, and national level Information Literacy Goals, Areas of Interest, Publications, Standards, etc." https://www.aahea.org/

Association of American Colleges and Universities (AAC&U): Aims "to advance the vitality and public standing of liberal education by making quality and equity the foundations for excellence in undergraduate education in service to democracy." https://www.aacu.org/

American Association of University Professors: Since its founding in 1915, "the AAUP has helped to shape American higher education by developing the standards and procedures that maintain quality in education and academic freedom in this country's colleges and universities." https://www.aaup.org/

Association on Higher Education and Disability: Since 1977, AHEAD membership represents "disability resource professionals, student affairs personnel, ADA coordinators, diversity officers, AT/IT staff, faculty and other instructional personnel, and colleagues." https://www.ahead.org/home

Campus Consortium: Has over 37,000 members representing higher education institutions and K–12 school districts. Its goal is to "help members reduce the time, cost, and effort associated . . . adopting new education technologies." https://www.campusconsortium.org/

Consortium for Student Retention Data Exchange at the University of Oklahoma: Two-year and four-year institutions dedicated to achieving the highest levels of student success through collaboratively sharing data, knowledge, and innovation. https://csrde.ou.edu/

EDUCAUSE: "Community of IT leaders and professionals working together to tackle challenges and leverage opportunities that are constantly evolving within higher education." https://www.educause.edu/

HigherEd Web Professionals: An international organization of professionals working to design, develop, manage, and map the future of digital in higher education. https://2020.highedweb.org/about/

International Society for Technology in Education (ISTE): "Inspires educators worldwide to use technology to innovate teaching and learning, accelerate good practice and solve tough problems in education by providing community, knowledge and the ISTE Standards,[1] a framework for rethinking education and empowering learners." https://www.iste.org/about/about-iste

Instructional Technology Council (ITC): "Represents higher education institutions in the United States and Canada and is a leader in advancing distance education." https://www.itcnetwork.org/membership-benefits

League for Innovation in the Community College: An international network of community colleges "with a mission to cultivate innovation in the community college environment." https://www.league.org/

National Association of Student Personnel Administrators (NASPA): An organization of student affairs administrators and professionals in higher education. https://www.naspa.org/home

National Association for College Admission Counseling: Provides "knowledge, networking and ethical standards for college admission professionals." https://www.nacacnet.org/about/overview/

NACADA: The Global Community for Academic Advising. It "promotes student success by advancing the field of academic advising globally." https://nacada.ksu.edu/

NAFSA: Association of International Educators. With "more than 10,000 members worldwide, NAFSA is committed to international education and exchange." https://www.nafsa.org/

National Collaborative for Digital Equity: http://www.digitalequity.us/index.html

National Student Clearinghouse® Research Center™: https://nscresearchcenter.org/aboutus/

The following conferences afford opportunities to engage with higher education innovators, educators, and administrators.

Bb World: https://bbworld.com/

InstructureCon: https://www.instructure.com/canvas/news/instructurecon2019/videos

Instructional Technology Council Annual elearning Conference: https://itc.eventbank.com/org/itcnetwork/events/

American Council on Education Annual Conference: Attracts "nearly 2,000 presidents, senior executives, and other higher education leaders from all institutional types to explore fresh perspectives for practical solutions on campus, network with top leaders across all higher education sectors, and bring data-driven insights back to campus." https://www.acenet.edu/Events/Pages/ACE2021.aspx

HighEdWeb 2020 Accessibility: "Online conference about digital accessibility in higher education." https://a11ysummit20.highedweb.org/#

Innovations conference: "Dedicated to improving organizational teaching and learning, and discovering new approaches for enhancing the community college experience." https://www.league.org/events

ISTE: Aims to accelerate the use of technology to solve tough problems and inspire innovation in education. More than 16,000 edtech leaders are set to attend ISTE 2020. https://conference.iste.org/2020/

Leadership in Higher Education Conference: https://www.magnapubs.com/leadership-in-higher-education-conference/

National Association for College Admission Counseling: https://www.nacacconference.org/

NAFSA eConnection: A multi-day digital conference. https://www.nafsa.org/conferences/2020-nafsa-econnection

NAFSA Annual Conference & Expo: A conference "dedicated to international education and exchange." https://www.nafsa.org/conferences/nafsa-2021

NASPA Annual Conference: "A global gathering of student affairs educators passionate about critical higher education issues." https://conference.naspa.org/

National Symposium on Student Retention (NSSR): "Explores the latest evidence-based research on post-secondary retention and graduation. The intimate, content-focused environment enhances the potential for networking and encourages collaboration among colleagues from diverse fields and institution." https://csrde.ou.edu/symposium/

Online Learning Consortium Accelerate conference: "Emphasizes the most innovative and impactful research and effective practices in the field of online, digital and blended learning." https://onlinelearningconsortium.org/attend-2020/accelerate/

Online Learning Consortium Innovate: Offers "hundreds of sessions spanning a wide variety of topics and special interest areas, including EdTech, proctoring, accessibility, gamification, K-12, open educational resources, and many more." https://onlinelearningconsortium.org/attend-2021/innovate/

Online Learning Consortium Collaborate: Scheduled regional events around the United States for online learning professionals, educators, and administrators to discuss "current and emerging trends in online learning, collaborate and network with your regional peers." https://onlinelearningconsortium.org/collaborate-overview/

United States Distance Learning Association conference: "The premier event for professionals in the distance learning industry." https://usdla.org/2020-national-conference/

The following technology provides platforms to streamline operations and enhance institutional student engagement.

Learning management systems[2] provide online platforms for the deployment of instruction. Among features: an LMS enables communication, attendance and grade tracking, student engagement and assessment.

Blackboard: https://www.blackboard.com/
Coursesites: https://coursesites.com/
Canvas: https://www.instructure.com/canvas/
Moodle: https://moodle.org/
D2L: https://www.d2l.com/
Open edX: https://open.edx.org/
Schoology: https://www.schoology.com/

TRACKING AND SUPPORT SYSTEMS

Advisor Trac: "Management and tracking solutions for advising, counseling that can link with your student information system to maintain accurate and up-to-date contact, demographic, and enrollment data from your registrar. Enables managing staff users across multiple centers"[3]

Ellucian CRM Advise: https://www.ellucian.com/solutions/ellucian-crm-advise.

Tutor Trac: Provides on-demand access to essential tools, such as appointment scheduling, logging visits, and activity reports.[4]

Smarthinking Online Tutoring: https://www.pearson.com/us/higher-education/products-services-institutions/smarthinking/for-students.html.

Starfish Retention Solutions: Early alert student intervention system. https://www.hobsons.com/solution/starfish/

OPEN EDUCATION RESOURCES

Community College Consortium for OER (CCCOER): https://www.cccoer.org/

MERLOT: An extensive collection of more than 90,000 learning open education learning resources. https://www.merlot.org/merlot/index.htm

OER Commons: A public digital library of open educational resources. https://www.oercommons.org/

OpenStax Textbooks: https://cnx.org/

FREE ONLINE COURSES

Open Learning Initiative: http://oli.cmu.edu/independent-learner-courses/
edX Free online courses from 140 institutions: https://www.edx.org/
Coursera: https://www.coursera.org/promo/free-courses-college-students
Saylor Academy: https://www.saylor.org/

DATA SERVICES

National Student Clearinghouse Services:

EnrollmentVerify: https://www.studentclearinghouse.org/colleges/enrollmentverify/

Student Tracker: https://www.studentclearinghouse.org/colleges/studenttracker/

DegreeVerify: https://www.studentclearinghouse.org/colleges/degreeverify/

Student Self-Service: https://www.studentclearinghouse.org/colleges/student-self-service/

REPORTS

2020 EDUCAUSE Horizon Report Teaching and Learning Edition: https://library.educause.edu/resources/2020/3/2020-educause-horizon-report-teaching-and-learning-edition

Extending XR across Campus: https://library.educause.edu/resources/2020/5/extending-xr-across-campus

AACC Competences for Community College Leaders, 3rd Edition: https://www.aacc.nche.edu/publications-news/aacc-competencies-for-community-college-leaders/

National Student Clearinghouse Research Center Reports

Current Term Enrollment Estimates: https://nscresearchcenter.org/current-term-enrollment-estimates/

Yearly Success and Progress Rates (national-level outcomes, a fifty-state data dashboard is available): https://nscresearchcenter.org/yearly-success-and-progress-rates/

Completing College National and State Reports: https://nscresearchcenter.org/completing-college/

NACADA Center for Research at Kansas State University: "Global think tank dedicated to research in academic advising and student success and serves as a resource for advancing the scholarly practice and applied research related to academic advising." https://nacada.ksu.edu/Resources/Research-Center.aspx

COMPANION TECHNOLOGIES

Accessibility Tools

Aira[5]: Through the Aira smartphone app blind and low-vision individuals can obtain instant access to visual information. Aira.io

Blackboard Ally[6]: An accessibility checker software that integrates with the learning management system and also provides alternate accessible content.

File Transformer[7]: Free Blackboard Tool that converts files to accessible formats such as HTML, electronic Braille, and ePub.

Concept3D.com[8]: Wheelchair accessible routes/interactive wayfinding platform for wheelchair users.

Verbit.ai: Verbit offers real-time transcription and captioning powered by artificial intelligence.

iBraille Challenge App[9]: "Through the app, using an iPad and a refreshable braille display, students can practice and hone their braille literacy skills."

iBraille keyboard: https://apps.apple.com/us/app/ibraille-keyboard/id1177830627

Refreshable Braille Displays: "Braille displays provide access to information on a computer screen by electronically raising and lowering different combinations of pins in braille cells. A braille display . . . changes continuously as the user moves the cursor around on the screen, using either the command keys, cursor routing keys, or Windows and screen reader commands."[10]

Screen Readers for the Blind:[11]

Openbook Magic: https://www.freedomscientific.com/products/software/openbook/

Job Access with Speech (JAWS): https://www.freedomscientific.com/products/software/jaws/

Zoom Text: https://www.zoomtext.com/

Read & Write: https://www.texthelp.com/en-us/products/read-write/read-write-for-education/

Reader Pens can scan text to upload to a computer. These pens also provide definitions and can read aloud:

C-pen: https://cpen.com/

ReaderPen: https://www.scanningpens.com/ReaderPenUS/#

NOTES

1. ISTE Standards Retrieved from https://www.iste.org/standards.

2. The 20 Best learning management systems. (2019). Elearning Industry. Retrieved from https://elearningindustry.com/the-20-best-learning-management-systems.

3. Trac Systems by Redrock Software Corporation. Advisor Trac. Retrieved from https://www.go-redrock.com/products/advisortrac/.

4. Trac Systems by Redrock Software Corporation. Tutor Trac. Retrieved from Retrieved from https://www.go-redrock.com/products/tutortrac/#:~:text=TutorTrac%20is%20the%20complete%20management,support%20students%20in%20higher%20education.

5. AIRA. How it Works. Retrieved from https://aira.io/how-it-works.

6. Blackboard Ally for LMS. Retrieved from https://www.blackboard.com/teaching-learning/accessibility-universal-design/blackboard-ally-lms.

7. Kelly, Rhea (2020, April 1). Free Blackboard Tool Converts Files to Accessible Formats. Retrieved from https://campustechnology.com/articles/2020/04/01/free-blackboard-tool-converts-files-to-accessible-formats.aspx?m=2.

8. Wilson, Colter. (2020, January 13). Wayfinding: Wheelchair Accessible Routes. Retrieved from https://campustechnology.com/articles/2020/04/01/free-blackboard-tool-converts-files-to-accessible-formats.aspx?m=2.

9. The Braille Challenge App. Retrieved from https://www.brailleinstitute.org/ibraille-challenge-app.

10. American Foundation for the Blind. Refreshable Braille Displays. Retrieved from https://www.afb.org/node/16207/refreshable-braille-displays.

11. American Foundation for the Blind. Screen Readers. Retrieved from https://www.afb.org/blindness-and-low-vision/using-technology/assistive-technology-products/screen-readers.

Bibliography

Akhtar, V. L. and Kotter, J. P. (2019). Charting the Course: The Path to Transformation in Education. Retrieved from https://www.kotterinc.com/research-and-perspectives/transformation-in-education/.

Aldridge, S. and Harvatt, K. (2014). *Wired for Success: Real World Solutions for Transforming Higher Education*. New York: American Association of State Colleges and Universities.

American Association of Community Colleges. Community College Enrollment Crisis: Historical Trends in Community College Enrollment. Retrieved from https://www.aacc.nche.edu/wp-content/uploads/2019/08/Crisis-in-Enrollment-2019.pdf.

American Association of Community Colleges. (2020, May 8). Prepare to Open: Strategies for Reengaging Students, Faculty, Staff, and Community After COVID-19 Webinar. Retrieved from https://www.aacc.nche.edu/2020/05/04/prepare-to-open-strategies-for-reengaging-students-faculty-staff-and-community-after-covid-19-webinar/.

Appreciative Advising. (2014). Retrieved from http://apps.nacada.ksu.edu/conferences/ProposalsPHP/uploads/handouts/2014/C224-H06.pdf.

Bailey, T., Jaggars, S. and Jenkins, D. (2015). *Redesigning America's Community Colleges: A Clearer Path to Student Success*. Cambridge, MA: Harvard University Press.

Berger, W. (2018). *The Book of Beautiful Questions*. New York: Bloomsbury Publishing.

Blankstein, M., Wolff-Eisenberg, C. and Braddlee. Student Needs Are Academic Needs: Community College Libraries and Academic Support for Student Success. *Ithaka S+R*. Last Modified 30 September 2019. Retrieved from https://doi.org/10.18665/sr.311913.

Bloom, J. L. The Appreciative Advising Revolution. Retrieved from www.ulm.edu/studentsuccess/advising/resources/bloom-advising.ppt.

Bloom, J. L. (2008). The Appreciative Advising Revolution. Retrieved from https://www.wssu.edu/academics/general-education/_files/documents/appreciative-advising.pdf.

Bolman, L. G. and Deal, T. E. (2008). *Reframing Organization: Artistry, Choice, and Leadership*. 4th Ed. San Francisco, CA: Jossey-Bass.

Bryk, A. S. and Schneider, B. (2003, March). Trust in Schools: A Core Resource for School Reform. *Educational Leadership* 60(6): 40–45.

Butler, Shai L. (2020, April 20). The Gift of Goodbye: Saying Goodbye to Normal and Hello to Extraordinary. Retrieved from https://www.higheredjobs.com/articles/articleDisplay.cfm?ID=2209&utm_source=04_20_2020&utm_medium=email&utm_campaign=ExecutiveInsiderUpdat.

Carey, K. (2015). *The End of College: Creating the Future of Learning and the University of Everywhere*. New York: Riverhead Books.

CCRC A framework for Advising Reform. (2019, July). Retrieved from https://files.eric.ed.gov/fulltext/ED597852.pdf.

Center for Community College Student Engagement. (2016). Survey of Entering Student Engagement (SENSE). Retrieved from http://www.ccsse.org/sense/survey/nationalbenchmark.cfm.

Center for Community College Student Engagement. (2018). *Show Me the Way: The Power of Advising in Community Colleges*. Austin, TX: The University of Texas at Austin, College of Education, Department of Educational Leadership and Policy, Program in Higher Education Leadership.

Centers for Disease Control and Prevention. Coronavirus Disease 2019 (COVID-19). Cases in the U.S. Retrieved from https://www.cdc.gov/coronavirus/2019-ncov/cases-updates/cases-in-us.html.

College Board. (2016, April). Trends in Community College Enrollment. Retrieved from https://trends.collegeboard.org/sites/default/files/trends-in-community-colleges-research-brief.pdf.

Conley, B. (2019, September 6). The Great Enrollment Crash Students Aren't Showing Up. And It's Only Going to Get Worse. *The Chronicle Review*. Retrieved from https://www.chronicle.com/interactives/20190906-Conley?cid=trend_right_a.

Consumer Financial Protection Bureau. (2017, June). Effective Financial Education: Five Principles and How to Use Them. Retrieved from https://s3.amazonaws.com/files.consumerfinance.gov/f/documents/201706_cfpb_five-principles-financial-well-being.pdf.

Davis Educational Foundation. Summon on Cost in Higher Education October 20–21, 2013. Retrieved from http://www.nebhe.org/info/pdf/events/conference/october2013/SCHE_Key_Themes.pdf.

Dima, A. M., Clodnițchi, R., Istudor, L. and Luchian, I. (2019). Business Excellence Models in Higher Education—Innovative Solutions for Management Performance. *Proceedings of the International Conference on Business Excellence* 13(1): 38–46. Retrieved 9 March 2020, from https://doi.org/10.2478/picbe-2019-0005.

Evolllution.com. (n.d.). Students as Customers: The New Normal in Higher Education. Retrieved from https://evolllution.com/attracting-students/customer_service/students-as-customers-the-new-normal-in-higher-education/.

Gallup-Purdue Index Report. (2015). Great Jobs, Great Lives: The Relationship Between Student Debt, Experiences and Perceptions of College Worth. Retrieved from http://www.gallup.com/services/185924/gallup-purdue-index-2015-report.aspx.

Gannon, K. (2017, February 27). The Case for Inclusive Teaching. *The Chronicle for Higher Education*. Retrieved from https://www.chronicle.com/article/The-Case-for-Inclusive/242636?cid=at&utm_source=at&utm_medium=en&elqTrackId=1500abcae2304617918ecd89e2f059d7&elq=be73f93a179e4d3bab3c40d3121b8b66&elqaid=18039&elqat=1&elqCampaignId=8019.

George, B. (2015). *Discover Your Truth North: Becoming an Authentic Leader*. Hoboken, NJ: John Wiley & Sons, Inc.

Georgetown University Center on Education and the Workforce, The Overlooked Value of Certificates and Associate's Degrees: What Students Need to Know Before They Go to College, 2020. Retrieved from https://1gyhoq479ufd3yna29x7ubjn-wpengine.netdna-ssl.com/wp-content/uploads/CEW-SubBA.pdf.

Gierdowski, D. and Galanek, J. (2020, June 1). ECAR Study of the Technology Needs of Students with Disabilities, 2020. *EDUCAUSE Review*. Retrieved from https://er.educause.edu/blogs/2020/6/ecar-study-of-the-technology-needs-of-students-with-disabilities-2020.

Gillispie, Brian. (2003). History of Academic Advising. *NACADA Clearinghouse*. Retrieved from https://nacada.ksu.edu/Resources/Clearinghouse/View-Articles/History-of-academic-advising.aspx.

Girma, Haben. (2019). *Haben: The Deafblind Woman Who Conquered Harvard Law*. New York: Twelve.

Goldstein, L. (2003, October). High Tech, High Tab: Alternative Approaches to Funding. *NACUBO Business Officer*. Retrieved from http://www.campus-strategies.com/downloads/books_articles/high_tech.pdf.

Goldstein, L. (2005, March). College & University Budgeting: An Introduction for Faculty and Academic Administrators, Third Edition. Retrieved from http://www.campus-strategies.com/downloads/books_articles/the_flexible_budget.pdf.

Griffiths, R., Mislevy, J., Wang, S., Ball, A., Shear, L. and Desrochers, D. (2020). *OER at Scale: The Academic and Economic Outcomes of Achieving the Dream's OER Degree Initiative*. Menlo Park, CA: SRI International.

Grigely, J. (2017, June 27). The Neglected Demographic: Faculty Members With Disabilities. *The Chronicle of Higher Education*. Retrieved from https://www.chronicle.com/article/The-Neglected-Demographic-/240439.

Guilbault, Melodi. (2016). Students as Customers in Higher Education: Reframing the Debate. *Journal of Marketing for Higher Education* 26(2). Retrieved from https://doi.org/10.1080/08841241.2016.1245234.

Hain, P. (2019, May 20). College Enrollment Declines Continue. Inside Higher Ed. Retrieved from https://www.insidehighered.com/quicktakes/2019/05/30/college-enrollment-declines-continue.

Harney, John O. 2013. "Exploring Higher Education Business Models (If Such a Thing Exists)." *New England Journal of Higher Education*, October 1.

Hendricks, R. (2017, December). Secretary's December 2017 Column 'The Equity Imperative': We Are All Important to New Jersey's Future. Retrieved from https://njsecretaryhighereducation.com/2017/12/01/dec2017-secretaryscolumn/.

Hevel, Michael S. (2016, October). Toward a History of Student Affairs: A Synthesis of Research, 1996–2015. *Journal of College Student Development* 57(7): 844–862

(Article). Johns Hopkins University Press. Retrieved from https://doi.org/10.1353/csd.2016.0082.

Hyman, C. L. (2018). *Reinvention: The Promise and Challenge of Transforming a Community College System*. Cambridge, MA: Harvard Education Press.

Joslin, Jennifer E. (2018). The Case for Strategic Academic Advising Management. *New Directions for Higher Education* 184(2018): 11–20. Retrieved from https://doi.org/10.1002/he.20299.

Kautz, T., Heckman, J. J., Diris, R., Ter Weel, B. and Borghans, L. (2014). Fostering and Measuring Skills: Improving Cognitive and Non-Cognitive Skills to Promote Life Time Success. Retrieved from http://www.oecd.org/education/ceri/Fostering-and-Measuring-Skills-Improving-Cognitive-and-Non-Cognitive-Skills-to-Promote-Lifetime-Success.pdf.

Khine, Myint. (2016). Non-Cognitive Skills and Factors in Educational Success and Academic Achievement. https://doi.org/10.1007/978-94-6300-591-3_1.

Klempin, S., Kalamkaria, H. S., Pellegrino, L. and Barnett, E. (2019, July). A Framework for Advising Reform. CCRC Working Paper No. 111. Retrieved from https://files.eric.ed.gov/fulltext/ED597852.pdf.

Kotter, J. and Rathgeber, H. (2005). *Our Iceberg Is Melting*. New York: Portfolio Penguin.

Kuh, G. (2008). High-Impact Educational Practices: What They Are, Who Has Access to Them, and Why They Matter. Retrieved from https://www.aacu.org/leap/hips.

Lynch, J. and Lungrin, T. (2018). Integrating Academic and Career Advising Toward Student Success. *New Directions for Higher Education* 184(Winter 2018): 69–79. https://doi.org/10.1002/he.20304.

Ma, J., Pender, M. and Welch, M. (2019). Education Pays 2019: The Benefits of Higher Education for Individuals and Society. Trends in Higher Education Series. *The College Board*. Retrieved from https://research.collegeboard.org/pdf/education-pays-2019-full-report.pdf.

Matson, T. and Robinson, J. (2018, April 5). Using a Strengths-Based Approach to Retain College Students. *GALLUP*. Retrieved from https://www.gallup.com/workplace/236063/using-strengths-based-approach-retain-college-students.aspx.

McGhee, Patrick. (2015, March 31). Let Students Be Students—Not Customers. Retrieved from https://www.theguardian.com/education/2015/mar/31/students-not-customers.

McGowan, H. E. (2019, September 10). The Workforce Is Calling, Higher Education, Will You Answer? *Forbes*. Retrieved from https://www.forbes.com/sites/heathermcgowan/2019/09/10/the-workforce-is-calling-higher-education-will-you-answer/#5a83e3276f6f.

McNair, T., Albertine, S., Cooper, M., McDonald, N. and Major, T. (2016). Becoming a student-ready college: a new culture of leadership for student success. San Francisco, CA: Jossey-Bass.

Mellow, G. and Heelan, C. (2008). Minding the Dream: *The* Process and Practice of the American Community College. Blue Ridge Summit, PA: Rowman and Littlefield Publishers.

Mitchell, M., Leachman, M. and Masterson, K. (2016, August 16). Funding Down, Tuition Up. Retrieved from https://www.cbpp.org/research/state-budget-and-tax/funding-down-tuition-up.

Mitchell, M., Leachman, M. and Masterson, K. (2017, August 23). A Lost Decade in Higher Education Funding. Retrieved from https://www.cbpp.org/research/state-budget-and-tax/a-lost-decade-in-higher-education-funding.

Mitchell, T. (2019, March 11). Changing Demographics and Digital Transformation. *Educause*. Retrieved from https://er.educause.edu/-/media/files/articles/2019/3/er191101.pdf.

NACADA. (n.d.) Nine Condition of Excellence in Academic Advising. Retrieved from https://nacada.ksu.edu/Portals/0/Resources/Excellence%20in%20Academic%20Advising/documents/NineConditionsofExcellence.pdf.

National Center for Education Statistics. (2017, May). The Condition of Education. Retrieved from https://nces.ed.gov/programs/coe/indicator_cha.asp.

Ohrablo, Sue. (2018). *High Impact Advising: A Guide for Academic Advisors*. Denver, CO: Academic Impressions.

Pasquerella, L. (2019, September 19). Yes, Employers Do Value Liberal Arts Degrees. *Harvard Business Review*. Retrieved from https://hbr.org/2019/09/yes-employers-do-value-liberal-arts-degrees.

Pelletier, Kathe. (2019, October 14). Student Success: 3 Big Questions. *Educause Review*. Retrieved from https://er.educause.edu/articles/2019/10/student-success--3-big-questions.

Peterson, J. A. and Rudgers, L. M. (2018, January 2). Saddle Up: 7 Trends Coming in 2018. *Inside Higher Education*. Retrieved from https://www.insidehighered.com/views/2018/01/02/predictions-higher-education-coming-year-opinion.

Potts, R. and LaMarsh, J. (2004). *Master Change, Maximize Success: Effective Strategies for Realizing Your Goals*. San Francisco: Chronicle Books.

Pratt, T. (n.d.). Colleges and Universities Join Together to Survive Enrollment and Financial Problems. Retrieved from http://hechingerreport.org/colleges-and-universities-join-together-to-survive-enrollment-and-financial-problems/.

Pritchard, A., Li, J., McChesney, J. and Bichsel, J. (2019, April). Administrators in Higher Education Annual Report: Key Findings, Trends, and Comprehensive Tables for the 2018–19 Academic Year (Research Report). *CUPA-HR*. Retrieved from https://www.cupahr.org/surveys/results/.

Redden, E. (2017, November 13). Declining International Enrollments. Retrieved from https://www.insidehighered.com/news/2017/11/13/us-universities-report-declines-enrollments-new-international-students-study-abroad.

Sanaghan, P., Goldstein, L. and Jurow, S. (2001, May). A Learning Agenda for Chief Business Officers. Retrieved from http://www.campus-strategies.com/downloads/books_articles/learning_agenda_cbo.pdf.

Schanzenback, D. W., Nunn, R., Bauer, L., Mumford, M. and Breitwieser, A. (2016). Seven Facts on Noncognitive Skills from Education to the Labor Market. Retrieved from https://www.hamiltonproject.org/assets/files/seven_facts_noncognitive_skills_education_labor_market.pdf.

Schuman, Rebecca. (2015, May). College Students Are Not Customers a Political Shorthand that Needs to Die. *Slate.com*.

Shea Smith, K. (2013, July 26). The Inner Student: Kathleen Shea Smith at TEDxFSU. Retrieved from https://www.youtube.com/watch?v=meQSpp3YO9o.

Sibel, Ahi. (2018). Applying Business Models to Higher Education. *International Journal of Educational Administration and Policy Studies* 10(9): 111–122.

Siemens, George. (2006). *Knowing Knowledge*. Creative Commons.

Smith, Ashley A. (2018, March 13). The Persistence Project. *Inside Higher ED*. Retrieved from https://www.insidehighered.com/news/2018/03/13/oakton-community-college-builds-faculty-student-relationships-increase-persistence.

Soares, Louis, Steele, Patricia and Wayt, Lindsay. (2016). *Evolving Higher Education Business Models: Leading with Data to Deliver Results*. Washington, DC: American Council on Education. Retrieved from https://www.acenet.edu/Documents/Evolving-Higher-Education-Business-Models.pdf.

Soria, Krista M. and Stubblefield, Robin. (2015). Building a Strengths-Based Campus to Support Student Retention. *Journal of College Student Development* 56(6): 626–631. Retrieved from https://doi.org/10.1353/csd.2015.0056.

StrataEducation.org. Changing the Value of Education. Retrieved from https://www.stradaeducation.org/report/changing-the-value-equation-for-higher-education/.

Supiano, B. (2018, January 19). Can Colleges Engineer Relationships? *The Chronicle in Higher Education*.

The Editors. (2010, January 3). Are They Students or Customers? *The New York Times*. Retrieved from https://roomfordebate.blogs.nytimes.com/2010/01/03/are-they-students-or-customers/.

Thomas, Carolyn and McFarlane, Brett. (2018). Playing the Long Game: Surviving Fads and Creating Lasting Student Success Through Academic Advising. *New Directions for Higher Education* 184(Winter 2018): 97–106. Retrieved from https://doi.org/10.1002/he.20306.

Tinto, Vincent. (2006). Research and Practice of Student Retention: What Next? *Journal of College Student Retention: Research, Theory and Practice* 8: 1–19. Retrieved from https://doi.org/10.2190/C0C4-EFT9-EG7W-PWP4.

True Value: A New Model for Measuring the Value of Postsecondary Education by Listening to Americans: Survey of 340,000 Adults Informs Creation of Strada Education Consumer Value Equation, Providing New Insight into Learners' Needs and Priorities. *PR Newswire*, November 18, 2019.

University Business. (2018a, January). Intensified Focus on Cost Control and Student Success. *Outlook 2018*.

University Business. (2018b, January). Supporting Students from Admission Through Completion. *Outlook 2018*.

University Business. (2018c, January). Recruiting, Engaging and Retaining Generation Z: Strategies to Meet Changing Expectations.

Webley, Kayla. Rethink College: 3 Takeaways from the TIME Summit on Higher Education. Retrieved from https://nation.time.com/2012/10/19/rethink-college-3-takeaways-from-the-time-summit-on-higher-education/.

Wood, P. (2016, June 10). Students Are Not Scholars. National Association of Scholars. Retrieved from https://www.nas.org/articles/students_are_not_customers.

Zakaria, Fareed. (2015). *In Defense of a Liberal Education*. New York: W.W. Norton & Company.

About the Author

Alexandra Salas, PhD, is the dean of Innovation, Teaching & Digital Learning Excellence at Delaware County Community College. She holds a PhD in education, with a specialization in education technology from Walden University, a master's in political science from Queens College, and a bachelor of arts degree in journalism and French studies from New York University.

Dr. Salas's professional philosophy is grounded in leveraging the transformational power of collaboration to build sustainable learning communities and partnerships that fuel student advancement and enhance the pipeline of learners, future professionals, and leaders. Her background includes work as an education consultant, speaker, and facilitator. She also has extensive postsecondary teaching experience in traditional and online platforms. Higher education focus areas include: leadership, systems thinking, student success, globalization, technology, and innovation.

For more information, please visit: https://www.dralexandrasalas.com/

www.ingramcontent.com/pod-product-compliance
Lightning Source LLC
Chambersburg PA
CBHW030146240426
43672CB00005B/295